T0304393

THE
KIDS
ARE ALL
RIGHT

Parenting with Confidence
in an Uncertain World

BEN & GABRIELLE BLAIR

WORKMAN PUBLISHING
NEW YORK

Workman
Workman Publishing
Hachette Book Group, Inc.
1290 Avenue of the Americas
New York, NY 10104
workman.com

Workman is an imprint of Workman Publishing,
a division of Hachette Book Group, Inc.
The Workman name and logo are registered
trademarks of Hachette Book Group, Inc.

Design by Bonnie Siegler

The publisher is not responsible for websites (or their content)
that are not owned by the publisher.

Workman books may be purchased in bulk for business, educational,
or promotional use. For information, please contact your local bookseller
or the Hachette Book Group Special Markets Department
at special.markets@hbgusa.com.

Library of Congress Cataloging-in-Publication Data

Names: Blair, Ben, author. | Blair, Gabrielle Stanley, author.
Title: The kids are all right : parenting with confidence
in an uncertain world / Ben & Gabrielle Blair.
Description: First edition. | New York : Workman Publishing, [2024] |
Identifiers: LCCN 2024024227 (print) | LCCN 2024024228 (ebook) |
ISBN 9781523526505 (paperback) | ISBN 9781523528158 (epub)
Subjects: LCSH: Parenting. | Parent and child.

Classification: LCC HQ755.8 .B584 2024 (print) | LCC HQ755.8 (ebook) |
DDC 306.874--dc23/eng/20240620
LC record available at https://lccn.loc.gov/2024024227
LC ebook record available at https://lccn.loc.gov/2024024228

First Edition September 2024

Printed in the United States on responsibly sourced paper.

10 9 8 7 6 5 4 3 2 1

**To our favorite people in the world:
Ralph, Maude, Olive, Oscar,
Betty, and Flora June**

CONTENTS

INTRODUCTION

WHY WE DIDN'T WANT TO WRITE A PARENTING BOOK

Hello there. We're the Blairs, Ben and Gabrielle. We're here to give you permission to quit Little League, to think differently about screen time, and to let go of the stress about your kid getting into college. We've been married since 1995, and we have six kids—four of them are eighteen years old or older, so technically, we have raised four kids, and are raising two more. By the time this book comes out, we will be down to one kid under eighteen.

Ben did his graduate work at Columbia University, earning a PhD in Philosophy & Education, and is currently the president and cofounder of Newlane University, an online university. Gabrielle graduated with a degree in graphic design and was one of the OG mom bloggers back in the aughts with her blog, *Design Mom*. She's maintained an influential public presence through her writing since 2006 and is the author of two books, both *New York Times* bestsellers—*Design Mom: How to Live with Kids*, and *Ejaculate Responsibly: A Whole New Way to Think About Abortion*.

When you're a parent of six *and* in higher education *and* the creator of an online community of millions of readers, most of whom are parents, you field a lot of parenting questions. Over the years we've heard from thousands and thousands of fellow parents who have shared their questions, concerns, dilemmas, and worries. Questions that have become more and more urgent.

Parents today are worried. They really want to get it right, and to get it right from the very beginning. We've heard it all: *Am I feeding my baby correctly? Is my toddler getting enough educational play? What if my child didn't get into our preferred preschool? Do I need to take a second job to afford a house in the neighborhood with the best elementary school? Are my kids getting enough family time? Is my child participating in enough extracurriculars? Are they taking enough AP classes? Do they have enough friends? Are they getting too much screen time? What if they don't get into a good college? What should they major in?*

Of course, most of these questions are ones we're unable (or unqualified) to answer. We're not perfect parents and we're definitely not clinical experts. So why do people keep asking us for advice? We think it's because we represent a safe forum where parents can voice their worries and concerns, and because people (whether they know us in real life or just through our online presence) can see how much we enjoy parenting. They can see that we've built a family culture that prizes adventure, creativity, and togetherness. They can observe that our kids actually like one another, that they enjoy spending time as a family, that they are smart and talented, confident and independent. They see college degrees from impressive universities. They see that we've disrupted our kids' schooling, but somehow our kids have gotten a good education despite those complications.

But we never wanted to write a parenting book.

For one, parenting is deeply personal. When someone comes to us to ask for parenting advice, it feels like there's no way we can get it right. We don't know their child, we don't know their marriage or partner (or not-partnered) situation, we don't know their finances, we don't know their health status, we don't know how they were raised. It feels so fraught—the chance of us offending them instead of helping them seems so high. And then there's the issue that too often, what's hard about parenting is not personal at all—it's systemic.

No parenting book is going to give you universal basic income, better childcare options, flexible work hours, an engaged co-parent, a supportive workplace, a well-funded school, or a tight-knit community. Any *one* of which would immediately lighten a parent's burden—and certainly more than any book could.

So again, we didn't want to write a parenting book. At the same time, we know so many parents like us are overwhelmed, hungry for advice, and obsessing over any parenting decision where it feels like we can assert some control—second-guessing what activities we sign our kids up for, responding to mistakes (real or perceived) that our kids make, fearing the unknown (will my kid have a successful career?), making choices based on our own childhoods because that's all we know, worrying when our kids seem out of step with their peers, making major sacrifices to access specific schools, camps, programs, coaches, etc., and dealing with the impossible standards the world puts on our kids, and on us as parents.

We know because we've been there ourselves. But in the twenty-seven years we've been parents, we can tell you that in our experience, the idea that any of these parenting decisions are high stakes is all a big myth. A big lie. And the stress about these decisions gets in the way of a lot of the important stuff.

We didn't set out to forge an unusual parenting path, but soon after we became parents for the first time, we found that we saw the best outcomes by reacting to what was actually happening, instead of worrying about what we thought *should* happen, or what other people would think about what was happening. And those reactions led to some unconventional choices.

Our path has involved moves from New York to Colorado to France to California and back again to France. (Waving hello from Normandy as we type.) Our path has involved developing careers that allowed us the flexibility to work from home years before "remote work" was even a thing. Our path has involved three of our kids skipping their senior years of high school—and missing prom and other senior-year rituals that seemed so important in our own childhoods.

We know that this unconventional path is not available—or even the best choice—for every family. But we also know that in forging our own path, we've inadvertently avoided many of the stresses, anxieties, and traps that seem to be a hallmark of modern parenting.

So why *didn't* we get stressed out about schools? Why *are* our kids so independent? *Was* moving abroad worth the effort? Why *didn't* we get bogged down in "getting it right"? We've spent a lot of time looking back to understand (in hindsight) whether this was all just the "luck of the Blairs" or whether there was some overarching philosophy or wisdom that could be extracted and shared with other parents. We've come to the conclusion that yes, there were a couple of significant shifts in our thinking that set the foundation for how we parented—and that they could shift your thinking too.

And that's why we decided to write a parenting book.

The first major shift was to reject the idea that there is a "reliable path to success"—that if we follow specific steps along a specific educational path, our kids are guaranteed prosperity and happiness. And that our main job as parents is to do whatever it takes to keep our kids on that path.

The second big shift we made was to realize—and accept—that our child is not us, and our childhood is not their childhood. This means constantly reminding ourselves that our kids are their own people and the world they live in is different from the world we grew up in.

These shifts were not easy to make, but they have become guiding principles for us. Whenever we find ourselves worried about a child or facing a tough parenting decision, or when we're knocking heads with one of our kids and can't seem to see eye to eye, it's almost always because we've lost sight of one of these two guiding principles. We may feel panicked as our child seems to be veering away from the reliable path to success and we're worried about their future. Or our child is resisting a decision we've made for them based on what is familiar to us, or what we would have wanted when we were young, instead of what actually makes sense for them in this moment of their own particular childhood.

As soon as we remember to bring the guiding principles back into focus, suddenly we are able to see the situation more clearly, the stress diminishes, and we can respond to the issue without fear.

In the pages that follow, we have tried to spotlight a variety of scenarios or questions that send us back to these guiding principles. We also want to share other things we learned as we shifted away from more familiar models of parenting: how we encourage independence while prioritizing shared experiences; how we make time for music and sports without letting activities take over our lives; and generally why we take the long view about this parenting thing, because we're not just raising kids for eighteen years, we're building relationships that we hope will last a lifetime.

We also hope to provide a portrait of the unusual but wonderful path we have taken as parents. Admittedly, as we build this portrait, we focus on positive outcomes, and we know that focus might make it seem like parenting has been really easy for us. But you already know that nothing about raising a family is "easy." Our parenting story has been characterized by experimentation, trial and error, decisions prompted by financial or psychological necessity, thrilling moments, glorious and challenging years, failures, backtracking, path switching, fits, starts, varying levels of anxiety and tension, hope, and despair. But life as a parent is like that. And our experiences and conversations with other parents suggest this is the rule more than the exception.

Now that the season of intensive hands-on parenting is largely behind us, we're in a position to look back and really evaluate what worked. So, we want to share what we've learned. We want to offer what we wish we had known earlier. Ultimately, we are writing this book to help calm your worries, to try to reassure you that whatever the parenting challenge you're facing, it's probably not your fault. And despite the challenges you feel today, and the worries you may carry about the future, there is reason for a lot of hope and a lot of joy in parenting—and it starts with shifting your mindset about some of the stresses and expectations you bear as parents.

We have loved being parents. It has challenged and stretched and transformed us. It has been beautiful to share a life with each child through ups and downs and witness each become their own person. We have really enjoyed it. We enjoy it still! And we believe our ideas can relieve some of the pressures and burdens of modern parenting, so you can enjoy it as well.

We hope you'll conclude, as we did, that there are many paths to a fulfilling life. The future looks bright, and the kids are all right.

1

STEPPING OFF THE RELIABLE PATH TO SUCCESS

HOW TO LET GO OF THE RELIABLE PATH TO SUCCESS (THAT IS NO LONGER VERY RELIABLE)

In order for you to succeed

as a parent, your child needs to succeed. And in order to do this, they need to be exposed to Mozart in the womb, and be reading by age four so they can excel in preschool, so they'll make it into a good elementary school, so they'll be accepted in a high-achieving middle school, so they can attend an impressive high school, where they should take a large number of stressful AP classes, and participate in plenty of time-consuming extracurriculars, and then go through the brutal and humbling process of college applications, so they'll be accepted into a respected university, which will lead to an important job, which means they will have a successful life.

Sound familiar?

Even if you have never thought or said the words "the reliable path to success," we feel confident that you have made major life decisions, for both yourself and your children, based on a belief—conscious or not—that there is, in fact, a *reliable path to success*.

This belief can inform where we choose to live, what activities we do with our children, what activities we have our children do on their own, what stressors we are willing to subject our children to, what expenses we are willing to incur, what sacrifices we are willing to make to fund those expenses, whether we get anxious or concerned about our child's behavior or performance, how we structure time and space in our homes—the list goes on and on.

The idea that there is a reliable path to success is the backdrop for many (maybe most?) books about parenting children and teens. It explains the multimillion-dollar test-prep industry. It explains government-sponsored college savings accounts and incentives. It explains the increasing costs of college—and the amount of crushing debt parents and children are willing to take on. Because how could you ever cap the value of the certainty that the reliable path to success promises?

For a good part of our parenting lives, we totally bought into it.

When our family was just starting out, we lived in a suburb of New York City for eight years. In those years, we made so many parenting decisions that were based on our ideas about the reliable path to success. We toured multiple preschools, then poured over our budget trying to figure out if we could afford the "best" one (we couldn't). We worried about which sports we should get our kids involved in. We agonized over when it would be most advantageous for our kids to start kindergarten. We researched the best age to start taking music lessons and started our kids as early as we could. We fretted that our kids didn't have the opportunity to do language immersion classes like some of their cousins who lived in other states.

We weren't alone in our concerns. We had a big social circle of fellow young parents, and these topics were *the* subject of conversation at every playdate and afternoon at the park. As our kids got older and were nearing the end of elementary school, the tenor of these conversations became even more solemn and serious. The local elementary school in our blue-collar town was considered "good enough," but would we really be enrolling our kids in the local middle school and high school? Our peers started moving their young families to more expensive neighborhoods and villages. They made huge sacrifices—years of eighty-hour workweeks—to afford to buy houses or pay double the rent. The goal: to access school districts with the "best" schools—schools that would be a path to an Ivy League future. Those who stayed in our not-fancy neighborhood looked into private schools.

We couldn't afford to move to neighborhoods zoned for the highest-rated schools, or send our children to private schools, or invest funds in tutoring, or other academic support. But we believed that if we *could* afford to do those sorts of things, that we *should* do them; that the expenses would be easy to justify.

And then something changed. We were having a conversation with some peers from our church congregation about high schools in the area and what it would take for our kids to get into a good college. At the time of this conversation, none of us had kids over age ten, so college was almost a decade away. We were talking about Brigham Young University (BYU), a university owned by our church. BYU is ranked in the top twenty-five schools in the United States (as of 2024 it's #20 per *The Wall Street Journal*'s college ranking), so it's a high-quality education. It's also one of the most affordable, because the tuition is subsidized by the church. As a result, getting kids into BYU was (and still is) a goal for many of our fellow church members. One mother said, "Well, for BYU, I looked into it and GPA is the main determining factor for admittance—it's weighted much heavier than ACT scores or extracurricular activities." (From what we understand this is still the case, with students encouraged to have a minimum of 3.86 to apply.)

Something didn't add up to us. Why were our church peers making big sacrifices to access the "best" high schools when those schools were known for being extremely challenging and competitive and had a reputation for burning out their students? If they wanted their kids to reach for BYU, wouldn't the smarter strategy be to attend whatever high school would enable their child to get the best GPA with the least amount of stress? For the first time, we caught a glimpse of how compelling the idea of the reliable path to success is for parents. Even though it was unnecessary for acceptance into BYU, parents were making big sacrifices to move to the "best" neighborhoods, with the "best" schools—schools that had a reputation for delivering a really stressful high school experience for their kids—in order to stay as close as possible to the mythical reliable path to success. When the easier path to a good GPA was available, parents deferred to the reliable path (attending the "best," and hardest, school) even when it risked hurting their child's chances of achieving the actual goal.

In hopes of finding clarification, we started to explore "paths to success" more intentionally. We spoke with friends and colleagues in Manhattan who were working at the top of their fields. Some had horror stories about their competitive prep-school experience and the debilitating pressure they felt to get into an Ivy League school. But clearly their hard work and stress-filled high school experience had paid off—they landed at places like Princeton for their undergraduate degree and then on to Yale for law school.

But we also spoke to friends who were working at the top of their fields who had gone to middling public high schools in midsize cities or small towns in the Midwest and West; public high schools that were practically the opposite of the East Coast prep schools. We'd hear how they'd skied every weekend, how they'd coasted through high school getting fine but not great grades. They got into their state university with little effort, buckled down and got serious about their schoolwork, and got into a respectable law school—not Yale, but a school in the Top 40—and then ended up at the same prestigious law firms, just like their stressed-out prep-school counterparts.

The reliable path to success insists that it's got to be stressful all the way from preschool to the big job. The kid needs to be stressed, and the parent needs to be stressed too. They need to be hyperfocused on the path the whole time. But when we examined this idea more closely, it fell apart. These people weren't anomalies—we knew a lot of people like this who had ended up with successful careers in competitive fields in New York City (investment bankers, corporate lawyers, advertising and media executives) without having educational stress or following the reliable path to success.

The more we looked, the more examples we noticed. Even outside the high-powered careers of Manhattan, it was still true—we met and spoke with so many people with fulfilling careers, that may or may not come with a big paycheck, but certainly met the definition of success, and who had achieved those careers without private school, without sacrificing a summer to study for the SAT, without following the reliable path to success.

The reliable path to success was *one* path, but it was not the *only* path, and for a lot of children, it isn't necessarily the best path at all.

We started to notice how much time we spent worrying about getting our kids on the reliable path to success and keeping them there. Why did we second-guess our kids' schools, even though we liked the school culture and our kids reported loving their teachers? Why were we concerned if our child was behind on homework, or excited when they joined the mock trial team? Why did our calendar favor cross-country practices over family vacations? And why were we distraught when our child's high school play was canceled?

Was it because we were responding to our kids' feelings about these ups and downs? Or was it because we had elevated the stakes of run-of-the-mill school accomplishments and setbacks?

The reality is, we second-guessed a school we were otherwise delighted with because it had a less-than-stellar rating. We were excited about our daughter's leading role in mock trial for the great college essay that would come out of it. We were distraught when the school play was canceled, because it could no longer be added to a list of accomplishments (on another college application). And we were okay with a yearslong commitment to the cross-country team—even if that meant changing family vacation plans—because we knew experiences like that keep lots of doors open on the reliable path to success.

All the excitement and all the second-guessing were related to their ability to stay on the reliable path to success.

It's been fifteen years since we started questioning the value of the reliable path to success and ultimately rejected it as a guiding force for how we raise our kids. But even if we hadn't rejected it, even if we had embraced it, in those fifteen years *that path has become less and less reliable*. Graduating from a top high school doesn't guarantee acceptance into your first-choice university. Straight As and a 4.0 isn't enough. The acceptance rate at Ivy League schools is around 5 percent. And even if your child gets in, the price may be a dealbreaker—the average cost for one year at an Ivy League school is over eighty thousand dollars. All the work and sacrifice to get into the best schools, so much stress on students that there is a suicide epidemic at "good" high schools, and still, it's no guarantee your child will end up at Harvard. Plus, the world is changing so quickly that even if or when your child graduates from a top university, you can't be confident a job will be waiting for them.

And then there are the emotional costs for the kids. Are they miserable? Are they stressed out? Are they on the path because they want to be, or because it pleases you, their parents? And for the kids who fall behind, there are endless arguments to buckle down, cajoling to finish homework, to take their work seriously—is the cost to the parent-child relationship worth it? And let's say your kid makes it to Harvard, graduates, and gets the big job. Does that equal success? Does it mean your child, now an adult, will be happy? Did they enjoy their path to the big job? Do they actually enjoy the big job itself? When they see the life of someone who has climbed the career ladder, are they seeing a life they want? Looking back, will they think staying on the path was worth it?

We could say that parents should, and usually do, seek out the best for their children. But these days, it seems that "the best" conjures a very narrow and limited portrait.

Once you acknowledge the limitations of the reliable path to success, it's a whole lot easier to step off the path when it's not making sense for your child or your family.

Once we rejected the reliable path to success as a guide for our family, parenting decisions became a thousand times less fraught—we could deal with what was actually happening, and what our child needed right then, instead of worrying about trying to construct or preserve a future that may never be, or that our child may not even want.

WHAT TO DO WHEN
SPORTS
BECOME A
PART-TIME JOB
AND YOUR KID HATES
PIANO LESSONS

The first summer after we moved to New York, we signed our son up for Little League. From what we could tell, it seemed to be the main extracurricular activity for five- and six-year-old boys in our community. It wasn't required in our social circle, but it was expected. And honestly it was familiar. Ben's childhood was essentially centered on sports—basketball, football, baseball, and soccer from preschool age up to middle school and then focusing on tennis in middle school and high school, while still casually playing team sports with friends and through church leagues. Gabrielle had little to no interest in sports as a child, and yet her parents signed her up for parks and rec softball teams through most of elementary school. It was just what was done in her family and community.

So we signed up our son for his first baseball (T-ball) team without thinking much about it. But not even halfway into the season, the questioning began. Gabrielle found the experience of having a child on a T-ball team maddening.

The biggest frustration was how much time it required—between practices and games (and prepping for the practices and games—snacks, clean uniform, driving back and forth) we were easily spending six or more hours per week on this activity. We had to structure every Saturday around these games—goodbye lazy mornings with the kids, making pancakes while they watched *Power Rangers* VHS tapes; instead we had to get everyone up and dressed and out the door for the next game. At the time, we had three very young kids, so the choice was either split up and send one parent and the T-ball player to the game, while everyone else stayed home (this meant losing out on our precious weekend family time), or taking the whole family and trying to keep the baby and toddler entertained through a very boring and always too-long T-ball game. Both felt like losing options.

It wasn't just the time issue, though, it was also the whole culture around it. These were such *little* kids, but so many of the participating families took this activity very seriously. They knew that even at that young age, kids were already being sorted into skill levels for future competitive teams, so they didn't really want more casual players on their teams—they wanted everyone to treat T-ball as an important and necessary activity. To miss a game, to lose a game, to arrive late to a game was to be the object of concern from the coaches and other parents.

Our son seemed to enjoy T-ball, but that didn't mean much, because he enjoyed every activity. A trip to the library or park or a playdate with a friend or building a LEGO set were all delightful to him. He was always happy to go to T-ball but was also equally happy to do any other number of activities.

And he certainly wasn't drawn to T-ball in a way that would suggest a future in baseball (as much as one can tell these things about a five-year-old). The idea seemed laughable.

After a couple of months of participation, Gabrielle started raising her concerns with Ben and the other parents. What was the point of this activity? What are the five-year-olds getting out of this? Is it worth the time and effort and resources we're dedicating to it? Is it fun? Are the kids enjoying themselves? Are the parents and family members enjoying themselves? Why have we all decided this is a good way to spend a weekend? Couldn't it just be a simple, fun activity? A chance for the kids to dress up like baseball players and try it out for a bit? Experience what a "team" is? Get a chance to feel what it's like to win or lose? Hang out with their friends and play a game?

Gabrielle started thinking about the families that were taking T-ball very seriously and hoped for more baseball in their child's future. What were they picturing? Each future team would take up even more time and energy than T-ball, because the games would get more serious as the kids' skills improved. The stakes for each game and each season would get higher and higher. Baseball would become a twenty-hour-per-week job for the family, a "job" they paid a lot of money to participate in. Did they understand that? Did they want that? And it's not just baseball, of course. Gabrielle could see families investing time and money—endless hours and thousands and thousands of dollars—in soccer, gymnastics, swimming, basketball, hockey, etc., and going out of their way to find special teams or particular coaches. Gabrielle was looking at these five-year-olds playing T-ball and wondered, did the parents think their five-year-old would eventually play baseball in high school? In college? On a professional team? Did they think their kid would earn a sports scholarship to pay for college?

Gabrielle started looking into it and learned that, statistically, these kids definitely won't go on to do any of the above. Very few Little League players go on to play in high school. A tiny percentage of high school players play in college. An even tinier percentage of college players end up playing professionally. Trying to guess or engineer your child's athletic future at age five just never made sense to Gabrielle.

Ben's high school had a renowned boys' basketball program, and they won many state titles. It was a big deal to play on the basketball team at Provo High. But looking back, he can think of only two players from his high school career who went on to play for Division I teams, and he doesn't know of any from any year who played for perennial powerhouse college basketball programs. And that's it. No professional players, and a tiny number of college players. And this is from a high school team where the athletes are spending hundreds and hundreds of hours training and practicing and playing!

We're not suggesting that the only reason to participate in sports is the prospect of playing professionally, or playing in college. But because of the commitment and resources sports often require, we needed to think more carefully about our involvement.

We decided we needed to come up with a more concrete approach to how our family would participate in sports. We started with a few questions: *Why do we want our kids to play sports? What are we hoping they get out of it?* For us, the answers were:

1) Sports are really important in America, and we want our kids to have basic cultural knowledge about the sports that are popular here. Along those lines, we want our kids to have a comfortable knowledge of baseball, football, basketball, soccer, and volleyball—ideally as both casual participants and viewers, but at least as viewers. (As illustrated in a later chapter about our child who wasn't interested in the rules of football, we don't pretend to have fully mastered this goal.)

2) We want our kids to have the experience of being on a team and to understand what it means to work together toward a shared goal, to rely on your teammates, to feel what it is like to win and lose, and to learn good sportsmanship.

3) We want our kids to have the experience of the discipline of practicing a sport and getting better at it, to see their skills improve and their body become stronger or faster or more flexible. We hope this will help them see their body as a useful tool they can use to enjoy physical activities and accomplish goals.

4) We want our kids to experience sports that they can participate in into adulthood—like tennis and running and swimming—so they can have ways to move their body at every age.

We've used these goals to guide our family participation in sports. To gain cultural knowledge of a particular sport, do they need to participate on a team, or will they get the chance to learn through their PE classes at school? When our kids asked permission to take a gymnastics class, we made sure to understand their goal: Did they want to do this as a social thing? Or did they see someone do a back handspring and want to learn how? Understanding that goal would help us decide how much time and how many resources we would put into a particular activity. If their friends moved on, so would they. If they learned the back handspring and wanted more, we'd stay.

Over the years we've had kids try T-ball, soccer, tennis, swimming, gymnastics, cross-country, and track and field. They've also tried a few days of snow-skiing lessons and wake-boarding lessons. And they've tried lots of different sports through school PE classes. In the United States, that included things like volleyball, dodgeball, baseball, and basketball. In France, it was activities like handball, Ping-Pong, badminton, kayaking, rugby, and swimming.

Of course, there are some kids who are truly passion-ate about sports. All they want to do is play basketball; they would work on basketball a hundred hours a week as it's end-lessly delightful to them. That's great! If you've got a sports system that you're happy with, we are so happy for you. But we want to tell the parents who have their kids signed up for sports and find that the whole thing is more of a burden than a blessing to their family that they have permission to opt out. You don't need to do this. You truly don't.

We know it's difficult to find low-stress, just-for-fun, team sport options in America. Joining a serious, competitive team is usually the only choice. Ideally, communities would have sport organizations where kids of all athletic abilities and ages could learn the basics of a team sport, have fun playing with their teammates in a low-stress setting, win some games and lose some games, and never feel like they have to earn their keep to be on the team. But in reality, in most communities, that's not how it works. If you have a twelve-year-old who wants to learn how to play soccer, they may be out of luck—their soccer-playing peers have probably already been playing for seven years or more and there may be no accessible or affordable options for true beginners. To us, that seems pretty crummy. People should be able to try a new sport at any age, and be a beginner at any age.

So what can you do instead? Put together a neighborhood sports camp for a few weeks in the summer, where it's just for fun, then parents (or a local teen-for-hire) could teach the basics of basketball, football, baseball, or whatever sports the kids are interested in. Maybe that turns into summer evenings of neighborhood families gathering to play a sport at the park. Or you could call the local parks department, and get this going on a community scale.

Depending on what your community offers, you could let your kids try lots of different sports without a big commitment. You could try a season of soccer and a season of basketball and a season of baseball. And if there's one they love, maybe you will continue. And if they don't love it, oh well, you can be glad they got the basics.

For us, the key has been to take a minute to ask: *What is it that we're trying to get out of this for our family and for our child in particular?* Having the answer to that question before you begin is huge and will make all the difference in how you approach the sport.

We've found these same questions and answers apply to music study and music lessons as well. Music lessons are a big-time commitment. They are expensive, they require specialized equipment and lots of learning materials, which are sometimes very difficult to find. They require regular practice to see improvement, but instead of practicing with a team like in sports, your child will likely be practicing on their own, which requires its own type of discipline. If your child isn't enjoying the lessons, or doesn't want to practice, it can turn into a stressful situation for a family. Sometimes, there's a straightforward fix—maybe your child needs a different teacher or would prefer learning a different instrument. Sometimes there is no apparent fix, and you give up.

Music can take over a family's life in the same way sports can, where it feels like a million hours of practice and lessons, while getting increasingly more expensive as you go along, and requiring going out of your way for more specialized teachers, or even a more specialized school. Like sports, most people who spend many hours on music lessons as a child may rarely even play music as an adult, much less professionally. So again, before diving into the world of music lessons, it's best to determine your particular *why*.

We both happen to care quite a bit about music, at least as much as we care about sports. So when we've felt overwhelmed with music lessons and wondered if it was a mistake, we've focused on our reasons for wanting our kids to participate in music:

1) We want them to understand how to read music. To us, that seems like an important life skill. In our communities—

family, church, school—there are so many opportunities to sing and play music together, and we want our kids to be able to do that comfortably. We think of it as a type of fluency that adds a lot of joy and value to people's lives. (Related: We think everyone should have access to music lessons and have tried hard to support the music programs in our public schools.)

2) We like the discipline and organization and creativity that learning music requires. As kids get better at their music and participate in band or orchestra, they are interacting with peers who have also developed discipline and organization.

3) There are all sorts of studies showing that learning music offers brain benefits. We don't pretend to be experts on this literature, but in our experience we like how music offers a way to think and experiment creatively and problem-solve through practice that is distinct from other activities.

4) We've never expected our kids to make music a career or a professional path (though they are welcome to do so), but what we have wanted is for our kids to reach enough musical proficiency so that they can participate in family jam sessions. By family jam session, we just mean hanging out with the family while singing and playing music together. And really that's it. If our music lessons deliver the family jam sessions outcome and nothing else, that's fine with us.

To be clear, very little proficiency is required for a family jam session, so mastering a particular instrument has never been the goal, though all the kids have advanced far enough in a particular instrument that they can play in a community band or orchestra.

We've tried lessons through private teachers and through public school programs. Our kids have taken lessons in cello, violin, piano, trumpet, trombone, clarinet, and oboe. We've also tried drum lessons. Interestingly, all six of the kids play some guitar (some play quite well, others just a few songs), but we never did formal guitar lessons; they mostly learned by looking up chords on YouTube. We have a ukulele and a mandolin at home, and the kids have tried those as well.

In an ideal world, kids would get to try several different instruments to discover what they like playing best. From a practicality standpoint, we like the guitar—it's portable and universal and you can often find an inexpensive one at garage sales.

We also think the piano or keyboard is a really helpful instrument for any family interested in music—it makes experimenting with music easy, even for beginners. We use it to accompany others, to tune instruments, to try composing new songs, to pick out a melody we want to learn, or just to play our favorite piano pieces.

Before you track down a teacher and invest in an instrument and begin music lessons, take a minute to think about what your goal is. Not what is the goal for the family down the street. What is *your* goal? What is your goal for your children? What is the outcome you're picturing? How long do you expect them to take music lessons? What is your plan if they don't like it? Do you want them to try two years of piano lessons and then see if they want to continue? Or like us, maybe you want your kids to be able to join in during jam sessions. So how far do they need to go music lesson–wise to get there?

Try to get really clear on what you want out of music lessons before you go, and then be flexible if things change. Most of our kids are young adults now, and when we look at our aims for sports and for music, we'd say we got closer to actually achieving our aims with music than with sports. But it doesn't matter. The guidelines helped us understand why we were spending our time the way we were. They helped us prioritize our family time, to feel less overwhelmed when trying to fit in lots of music lessons for lots of kids, and to not be hard on ourselves if our kids had to miss a gymnastics practice.

Things like music and sports—and other activities too!— can take over a family's life. That may or may not be a bad thing. If an activity has taken over your family's life and everyone is thriving and enjoying it, then high-five! Keep on keeping on. But if you've discovered an activity is taking over your family's life and you're resenting it, it's worth taking a minute to figure out what you really want out of the activity, and how you can accomplish those goals with a minimal burden to your family.

HOW TO HELP YOUR KID GAIN CONFIDENCE OR EXCEL AT SOMETHING

Ben's brother, Jim, has a theory about how people become really good at a new skill, a theory that he refers to as Low Stakes, High Frequency. Here's the idea: The best way to get good at something is to perform your skill publicly (meaning there's an audience), as often as possible, when there's very little—but not nothing—on the line. The theory is that consistent practice with just enough pressure to keep you focused (but not too much!) is the way to get good at something.

Our youngest three kids were members of a swim team while we lived in Oakland, California. The team was called the Temescal Tidalwaves, and it was such an excellent experience. Any kid or teen who knows how to swim can join the team, at any skill level. There is no tryout. It is inexpensive to join—fifty dollars for the whole summer (with waivers for those who don't have the budget). Practice is every day, Monday through Friday. Lots of kids show up daily, but some don't take it as seriously, and show up only a couple of times a week. Which is fine. No one is stressed out about it. Swim team is supposed to be fun, and it is.

There are lots of teams like the Temescal Tidalwaves all over Oakland, and swim meets happen every Saturday morning, with two or three teams matching up at a local pool. The pools are not fancy. The facilities are very basic; all are outdoors.

There is no seating, and no shade, so families of the swimmers bring folding chairs from home and pop-up canopies. There are no official timers, so parents take turns volunteering with hand timers, clipboards, pens, and paper. There is no snack bar, so everyone who can brings some food and puts it on a shared table for any kids to help themselves. Uniforms are too expensive for some swimmers, so there is little emphasis on matching suits or swim caps. Every kid who shows up gets to swim in the meet, in two or three races. There are no team captains. No rankings of the swimmers. No drama about who is on the relay teams.

Meets are short and very fun, with lots of team cheers and gentle rivalry. We would typically arrive home by midmorning, no later than 11:00 a.m., in plenty of time to make a late breakfast of pancakes. Winners of the races are not announced at the meet. There are no medals or ribbons at the meets. But the coaches know the times and can let the kids know if they had a particularly good race.

By participating in swim team our kids got quite good at swimming. They got good at swimming publicly and weren't stressed out by it. At the meets, they had lots of opportunities to watch other good swimmers from other teams and notice their techniques. They got lots of encouragement from team members and the parents of other team members. They wanted to do well and improve their time and get points for their team, but there wasn't really any pressure to do so. There were no negative consequences if they didn't improve their time, but they would naturally reflect on what was especially good or bad about their performance in a certain race.

At the end of the season, there was a team party at the pool. Coaches gave out a trophy to each participant and sweet/silly prizes like "most improved" or "best splash."

As you would expect, some exceptional swimmers have come out of these Oakland swim teams and have gone on to more intense training, and to swim competitively at the college level. But most are just regular kids who can confidently swim all types of strokes and will very likely enjoy swimming as a lifelong skill and a great way to exercise. And they got good at swimming with little to no stress. Because: Low Stakes, High Frequency.

Thanks to the Temescal Tidalwaves swim team, all three of our kids who participated are solid swimmers, strong in all four strokes, and when we moved to France and they started swim practice, they were immediately placed with the top swimmers.

Maybe the swim programs are similar where you live. Or maybe they are the opposite. There are lots of places where swim programs are intense, competitive, and exclusive. It's expensive to join. You must try out and not everyone makes the team. Meets go for eight hours or more, and have costly, involved timing systems, and families are expected to stay the whole time, so people really have to commit to it and make big sacrifices to participate. There are fewer swim meets because they take so many officials to staff and are expensive to run. And the kids who aren't top swimmers get fewer chances to participate in races during the meets.

Kids may get stressed that they are not good enough. There are medals and rankings at every meet. Parents get upset if their child isn't getting placed in the "best" races. When the kids do get to race, there's a ton of pressure, and it feels like a major loss if they don't do as well as they hoped.

These programs no doubt produce some excellent swimmers. But just like in Oakland, most of the kids will never go on to be competitive swimmers beyond high school. They're just regular kids, who may or may not be turned off by swimming altogether depending on how intense their program is. High stakes. Low frequency.

Ben's brother has four kids who play violin, viola, cello, and piano, respectively. And he's noticed that in some music programs, there are lots of chances to perform, and the performances are low stress. Families can come and go during the concert—you don't have to commit to sitting still for a full multihour program when your kid is playing one song near the end. The publicity leading up to the performances is simple—like a listing on a chalkboard. And the performances aren't fancy. They don't require a ton of staff or formal clothes. And because these more casual performances are easy to put on, they happen more often, and kids get lots of chances to be onstage and perform for an audience (even though it might be a small audience). Low stakes. High frequency.

But in other places, recitals are a big deal, and tend to be few and far between. The schools make a show of fancy concert posters and programs, and students get very limited opportunities to perform onstage, and if they mess up, it feels like the end of the world, because it may be another year before they are onstage again. Performing in front of others becomes an incredibly stressful activity. High stakes. Low frequency.

One last example we'll use is blogging. Gabrielle is a much better writer now than when she started a blog in 2006. At the beginning, she wasn't great, but that was okay. She published posts every day (high frequency), but only a few people were reading at the time, so if the post wasn't that good, oh well (low stakes). By the time she had a large readership, and her posts (and topics) felt more high stakes, she was a much better writer, and knew how to handle public responses (the good and the bad).

So, if you want to help your child get a solid foundation in a skill, or if you are looking to help your child get to the next level, the answer may not be to insist your child practices more or harder. There is actually a fairly simple formula: Work to lower the stakes and increase the frequency of the performances of whatever it is you want to help your child with.

HOW TO GET COMFORTABLE WITH A SCHOOL YOU'RE NERVOUS ABOUT

When we were moving from France to Oakland, Gabrielle wrote a blog post about this major change, and we immediately heard from lots of Bay Area locals. They sounded worried and told us to look up our assigned high school on a rating site called GreatSchools.org. So we did. The school was rated a two out of ten. We'll repeat that: two out of ten.

Two! Two? What does that even mean, we wondered. Is the school some sort of black hole of despair? Partially burned to the ground, with students desperately navigating through the smoking, charred remains? Has the National Guard been called out to patrol the campus? Is disease and ruin running rampant among the students? What in the world is a "two" school even like?

The week before school started, we visited the campus for the first time, for our daughter's freshman registration. This was the first US high school experience any of our kids would have. As we walked through the parking lot, we heard music playing in the quad (it was Michael Jackson), saw tents and tables set up for each of the different clubs and organizations, and joined the other nervous parents and nervous fourteen-year-olds who were not sure where to start.

Then the upperclassmen started welcoming the freshmen. The sports teams were enthusiastically recruiting; so was the debate team. Key Club and Build On were offering service opportunities for students and reminding them that service "looks great on your college applications." We heard more about the legendary theater department (Tom Hanks graduated from this high school and at one point generously donated funds to ramp up the performing arts program). The students we met were kind and confident. Despite its low rating, we could easily see there was plenty to love about this school. We met with the freshman counselor to go over a four-year plan for our daughter and we were impressed—the counselor was young, and she herself was a graduate of the high school.

The district listed the school's demographic stats as 30 percent Hispanic, 30 percent Black, 30 percent Asian/Other, and 10 percent white, which made it the most diverse of all our kids' previous schools. This also seemed to be an important indicator of why the GreatSchools.org score was so low—some of the students were immigrants and were still learning English, which affected the standardized test scores of the whole school (and brought the GreatSchools.org rating down). But with our recent move from France, we could commiserate with trying to attend school in a language you are still learning and appreciate how much value there was in having a lot of different languages spoken by a student body.

On those school registration days, we saw tons of parental support—a father or mother taking time off work in the middle of the day to attend with their child, and to make sure all the paperwork was in order. But there were definitely some kids who were navigating the registration system and paperwork on their own. We learned there were no school buses (we had district-owned yellow school buses in both New York and Colorado); instead, students traveled from all over the city, and they mostly used public transportation to get there (a handful drove their own cars). The campus was closed, meaning everyone ate lunch in the cafeteria. Lunch was very short (at least compared to France) and our kids would bring a sack lunch, but they said that was unusual, and that most kids would pick up something at school.

The campus is on prime property with amazing views of the San Francisco Bay. In fact, the houses surrounding the school had superhigh prices. But interestingly, the residents around the school generally wouldn't send their kids there and opted for private school instead.

Our conclusion: GreatSchools.org isn't doing anyone any favors by labeling a school with a two. It may be reflective of test scores, but ultimately it didn't tell us anything of real value. And it must have been a huge downer for the 1,800 students attending the school, and their families, if they were aware of it. More instructive to us? There was a list on the school website of the universities where students from the most recent graduating class were accepted. Pretty much every top university was on the list (yes, even Harvard). Our high schoolers had never mentioned an interest in Harvard, so we didn't actually care about that—but what it illustrated is that no door would be closed for our kids by attending this school. And when we heard positive details about the school culture from our kids, we felt confident that attending this school would be a fantastic educational experience beyond just the classroom.

Our son loved the opportunities the high school gave him. He enrolled as a sophomore and in that first fall, he tried out for the school play and won the part of the Italian father in *Golden Boy*. He also found opportunities in music. He played the trombone, so he joined the marching band and jazz band. He'd always been pretty casual about his trombone playing, but found he had to really practice in order to keep up with his bandmates. Joining the band challenged him and gave him experiences he couldn't have had any other way—the band performed in competitions around the state, parades around town, and even at a renowned jazz club in downtown Oakland. At the end of the year, he laughed when he received the award for "Most Improved Band Member."

Our daughter started as a freshman and was *so happy*. She really, really thrived at this high school. She joined the cross-country team right off the bat. This was her first opportunity to try distance running, and she had no idea how much she was going to like it. She was dedicated and practiced six days a week. If we were traveling and she had to miss practice, she would run laps around the hotel. As cross-country ended, she transitioned to the track team, and again, she loved it, especially working out and traveling with the team.

One thing that helped our kids integrate into the school right away was that they were superinvolved. Have you ever seen the extracurricular activities scene of *Rushmore*? It was like that—joining every club, participating in every possible activity. They show up in the yearbook at least a dozen times. Of course, some of that is just their personality, and not every student would want to be that involved. But it was good for us to see how many options and opportunities there were at the high school. Because they were so involved, at the end of the year, their peers recommended each of them for student leadership.

One fear of parents when looking at low-rated schools is wondering if their child will be challenged. Will the courses be rigorous enough, or will they be built around the lowest common denominator? Our kids seemed to experience some of both. There were serious classes like AP World History that challenged them. But there were also classes that felt like a review of earlier work, and still others that were being constantly disrupted and were frustrating. Certainly, some of this depended on the teacher.

Another fear parents often have for their children in a big public high school is wondering if they'll find good friends. And our kids definitely did. They found there were lots of ambitious kids trying their best—you could especially find them in the AP classes and in places like orchestra and band and cross-country. Our kids told us there were plenty of students aiming for top universities, and their friends landed at great schools: Berkeley, UCLA, Stanford, and Harvard.

Though our kids thrived, the school was not perfect. We mentioned disruptions during class, and that was a real problem. And there were other workarounds we had to figure out. For example, both of our kids took Advanced French, and the next class would be AP French, but not enough students signed up for it, so the school didn't offer it. Instead, we had to look at some online options. Sometimes there were fake bomb threats—the kids would all have to walk down to the football field until the threat was confirmed fake. Which it always was. Apparently, students would call in a bomb threat if they wanted a test to be canceled. That said, our kids didn't feel unsafe. Unlike many high schools in the United States, there wasn't a police presence, and there weren't metal detectors either.

Like many public schools, the school simply needed more funding—funds for a few more people to share the load of administration, funds for teachers so that the school could find and keep the best ones, funds for a robust grounds crew so the students could feel proud of their campus.

Our public elementary school experience in Oakland was similarly hopeful. Though while our high school got a two out of ten on GreatSchools.org, our elementary school got a six! Doesn't that sound superhigh when you compare it to a two?

We loved our elementary school. Not long before we moved there, budgets for California public schools had been slashed significantly, but the number of programs that were offered, especially considering the resources available, was incredible. The community of people who supported the school was also outstanding. Like the high school, the attendees of the elementary school were a diverse bunch—18 percent Hispanic, 30 percent Black, 20 percent white, 17 percent Asian, 14 percent "Other," and 1 percent Hawaiian/Pacific Islander. The school newsletter was published in not one, not two, not three, not four, but five languages!

A few perks and programs our school offered included the weekly, very informative newsletter, a choir with weekly practices and seasonal performances, a tribal drumming teacher, a robust art program with an artist in residence, and a school band. There was an annual Bike Day and a big art event during the fall. There was also a Fall Carnival—held during parent-teacher conferences so parents can attend while their kids are at the carnival—making babysitters unnecessary and boosting parent attendance (such a smart strategy). There was a big deal talent show in the spring. There was even a charming campus garden, growing food right before the students' eyes. All these programs were funded 100 percent by family donations to the school and administered 100 percent by volunteers. It was remarkable.

Along with those programs, there were community-building organizations attached to the school—like a dads group that hosted a welcome picnic for all school families at the start of the school year, and a Friends of the School group that handled ongoing fundraising.

All these programs were funded by relatively modest donations from families—parents who were able, were asked to donate three hundred dollars for each of their kids who attended the school (one kid = $300, two kids = $600, etc.). That's it. The fanciest private school in town was just a couple of blocks away, and tuition there was thirty thousand dollars per year, and parents were still expected to support fundraising efforts. We couldn't help but notice the contrast. Thirty thousand dollars per year to allow one child access to a school community versus three hundred dollars per year to fund programs that benefited all the kids in their school.

Clearly, the positive impact was so vast because many families donated or volunteered or got involved in some way. But when it came down to it, there were truly just a handful of people who were really making it happen behind the scenes. One of our big takeaways from our experience at the elementary school is confirmation that it doesn't take a lot of people to make a huge difference. A core group of parents committing to the school can change everything.

And it wasn't just the parents. The teachers in the school were incredibly resourceful. Our son's teacher took the kids on a field trip every month, but she was allotted zero budget for this, so each child brought in five dollars to fund the outing, and instead of a bus, parents volunteered to drive (a parent with a minivan could bring five or six kids, so it didn't require too many parents for any given field trip). If a family could pay more, they did—and that funded the kids who couldn't afford the five dollars. It was impressive to see what she provided the kids on such a small budget, including visits to the planetarium, zoo, and botanical gardens.

Would we have ever considered taking our kids out of the public schools? Sure. If we felt they were unsafe in any way, we would have found alternatives. And if they felt doors were closing—that they weren't able to learn what they needed to learn—we'd look at other options.

In fact, for a short period, we did just that. Our first year in Oakland, one of our kids went to a private school where she could continue her French language studies. And during our second year, two of our kids tried a charter school focused on the arts. We had great experiences at both of those schools but concluded we preferred the offerings at our local public schools. There are several reasons we prefer public schools, and one reason is this: At both the charter and private school, much more time and money was expected of families than at the public schools. And if a family can manage to give that much time and money to a school, the time and money will go much farther—and have a positive effect for far more students—at a public school than they will at a private or charter school.

If your family is about to make big sacrifices to afford private school, or if you live in a place where you feel like your kids can't attend the public schools because of low ratings, don't automatically dismiss the idea of your child attending your assigned public school. Before you reject a school based on its rating, visit the school and see what it is like. Talk to families whose kids attend the school. Talk to someone on the PTA and see if there is a core of involved parents. When you hear about "bad schools," picture the kids who attend, and then picture their parents. Remind yourself those parents love their kids as much as you love yours and they want what's best for their kids every bit as much as you do.

While we're on the topic, here's one more plug for public schools: Free public schools are vital and valuable. Functioning and healthy public schools are necessary for a functioning and healthy country. There's no getting around it. If you want your kids to live in an awesome country, then your best bet is to make sure every kid in your community (not just your own kid) gets an awesome education. And the simplest way to do that? Support your public schools.

HOW TO
LET GO OF
EXPECTATIONS
AROUND
HIGH SCHOOL
TRADITIONS

As of this writing, our youngest is in middle school, and our second youngest is in high school (both at a local French school here in Normandy). The older four kids? Their education paths have been very different. Put it this way: six kids, most of them already finished with high school and college, and so far, we've only attended two graduation ceremonies.

One son attended preschool and half a year of kindergarten in Colorado. When we moved, he attended the other half of kindergarten in France, plus first and second grade. He didn't speak a word of French when we arrived, and because of his age at the time, he learned French without ever really having to try. In kindergarten, you're still learning school-related vocabulary, and apparently it's just as easy to learn that new vocabulary in French as it is in English.

He started third grade when we moved to California—he attended our neighborhood public school. Coming back to American school was a rough transition—they write exclusively in cursive in France, but he wasn't allowed to use cursive at the school in Oakland. By fifth grade he had found his groove, was a class leader, and was asked to speak at the fifth-grade advancement celebration.

He started sixth grade at the neighborhood public middle school, and then attended a year at a charter school focused on the arts. It wasn't a negative experience, but it wasn't a good fit, and he was very happy to return to the public middle school. In eighth grade, he was valedictorian, and spoke at the eighth-grade advancement celebration.

Then we moved back to France where he started high school. But it had been six years, and he no longer had much of his French language skills. It was a rough first year of high school. He went from valedictorian to the bottom of his class overnight. He was struggling to relearn French in addition to the coursework of his challenging classes. And then the pandemic shutdowns started in the last half of his freshman year of high school. Suddenly he was home all the time and learning French slowed way down.

When he returned to school, he rallied and did well on the big French exams—the Brevet and the Baccalaureate. He wanted to attend an English-speaking program for university and applied in the United States, Ireland, and Australia. Ultimately, he decided to attend a creative writing program in Dublin and is thriving. He's joined five different clubs (they call them "societies"), is the "freshers representative" for two of them, tried out for the fall play, and was the only freshman to get a speaking part (he played the uncle in *Footloose*).

Notably, he was our first child to attend all four years of high school.

When we moved from France to Oakland, one daughter started her freshman year of high school at our local public school. She loved it and thrived. And we could see she was happy to be taking classes in her native language. She signed up for the cross-country team, she participated in student government and jazz band, took several AP classes, and got great grades. She was especially committed to cross-country and became the team captain her junior year.

We spent a few weeks back in France the summer after her junior year to reconnect with friends and revisit many of our favorite places. When we first arrived, she would run each day to try to keep up with her target cross-country pace. We also rented an electric piano so she could practice for the upcoming year of jazz band. Several weeks into this summer France trip, the four older kids and Ben went on a pilgrimage to Mont-Saint-Michel, walking about twenty kilometers a day over four days, sleeping in an abandoned farm, a gentle meadow, and the attic of an old stone abbey at night. They walked with a group of around twenty-five other pilgrims, and (as is customary) our daughter had some long conversations with many different pilgrims that changed her path.

Though shocking at the time, she decided not to attend her senior year, and instead, she moved to Paris to be an au pair. When she pitched this idea to us, of course we had many questions about the whys and hows of it all, but she had solid answers and a good plan. She was confident in her decision, and knowing how capable she was (and still is), we were supportive of this big change in direction.

While working as an au pair, she was tasked with speaking English to the boys she cared for, but despite that, a year in Paris with a French family really strengthened her French. She still had a few courses to take in order to graduate from high school, and we found online versions that would give her credit. That fall, from Paris, she applied for college. We helped her work on applications over video chat.

While in Paris, she also successfully completed her high school courses online, and arranged with her California high school to come back from Paris in June and "walk" during graduation. Note: This has been the only high school graduation that any of our kids has attended so far (and no, graduation ceremonies aren't really a thing in France).

Despite her unconventional path, she was accepted into the prestigious University of California, Berkeley (locals call it Cal) and majored in English. She graduated school in May 2021—Gabrielle flew out to celebrate with her, but of course, still deep into the pandemic, there was no actual ceremony.

When we moved to Oakland, we enrolled another daughter in an experimental French and Spanish immersion school for seventh grade—with the hope it would help keep our family connected to France. We couldn't afford the tuition but worked out a marketing-for-tuition trade for a hefty discount. After a year, we realized we preferred the Oakland public schools, and she enrolled at our neighborhood middle school. She quickly found a terrific group of friends—girls who became women she is still close with today.

At age thirteen, she wanted an adventure and arranged to move back to France for a semester, to live with a dear family friend, and attend the school she had attended before, so she spent the first half of eighth grade in France, without us, and returned significantly more independent.

She went on to attend our assigned public high school and thrived. She was Juliet in the school's production of *Romeo and Juliet*, she participated in several traveling plays; she was a lead in mock trial, led a voter registration drive, and was an activist and organizer speaking out about gun violence.

She then made arrangements to follow in her sister's footsteps and skip her senior year of high school to be an au pair, but in Montpellier, France. She took her remaining high school credits as online classes and left for France at the beginning of what would have been her senior year. While she was in Montpellier as an au pair, the pandemic lockdowns happened. We had been so worried she would miss out on senior year activities and graduation. Once again, we learned our worry was a waste—even if she had stayed in Oakland, she would not have experienced the usual senior year anyway.

For university, she knew she wanted to study film in France. She applied and was accepted to EICAR—a film school in Paris—where she finished her degree in directing. Her program was in French, and it was a thrill to see her doing college-level work in French.

One son attended preschool through fifth grade in New York. We distinctly remember so much anxiety about when he should start kindergarten—he had a late August birthday and the registration cut off was September 1; should we enroll him as the youngest in his class, or wait a year, and enroll him as the oldest in his class? In Colorado, he attended sixth grade and half of seventh grade. In France, he attended half of seventh grade, plus eighth and ninth grade. Learning French from zero was tough as a seventh grader, but he committed and became quite fluent.

When we moved to Oakland, he started at the local public high school as a sophomore. He joined a million clubs and got excellent grades. The following fall, he moved back to France for a semester on an informal student exchange with one of his friends and lived with a French family. His French markedly improved, and he became much more independent. When he got back to California, he was resistant to return to school. He felt he had gotten what he wanted out of high school and wanted to drop out and take the GED. We laugh now about all that unnecessary anxiety around when he should start school, but it never occurred to us he wouldn't finish school.

He later enrolled in community college, took two years off for a mission, and then returned and completed his required coursework. Then he transferred to Cal and earned his bachelor's degree in film. We were able to attend his graduation. (If you're curious, we talk a lot more about his route from high school dropout to Berkeley grad in the next chapter—it's a compelling story for anyone who is stressed out about college.)

This was the second of two graduations we've ever been able to attend.

Four different kids, four different educational paths. Three kids moving back to France independently, three college graduates and counting. Lots of moves, lots of different schools. What we learned: There are multiple paths to college, if that is important to you. There are lots of chances to start over. You can still attend an excellent university even if you drop out during junior year of high school. And if you want your kids to develop skills like confidence and independence, there are lots of unconventional ways to do that too.

Though you may not guess it from our experience, we believe there is a lot of value in the traditional high school experiences, rites, and rituals. We appreciate the community gathering and sense of renewal of school registration each fall. We value the cross-country and track-and-field meets where we have witnessed our children exert themselves and reach and work toward a goal. We love high school theater productions and the opportunities they provide for public performances to large audiences. And we love the experience of graduations, celebrating our children's accomplishments, the journey that has led to this end, and imagining their future now with their diploma. We love and deeply value the community camaraderie that exudes in all these occasions.

We value high school traditions, but we are also willing to let them go. Our children have gained valuable experiences by removing themselves from these traditions—experiences that have shaped them in positive ways.

You might have some nonnegotiables for your children, and maybe they include graduation or at least regular atten- dance at high school for four years. And you might be inclined to worry and get anxious if your child is not on that path or is threatening to opt off that path. Our experience suggests that the traditional path is familiar and can work for some children. But it is not the only path. If you and your child are locking horns over your insistence that your child follows this path, consider easing up. You don't have to let go of all expec- tations and values, but it's worth examining why you feel so attached to the known path. Our kids have left the path sev- eral times now. And it's been okay. Letting go might bring some welcome relief for both of you—and your relationship.

WHY YOU CAN STRESS LESS ABOUT YOUR KIDS GETTING INTO COLLEGE

We don't stress about our kids

getting into college, but that wasn't always the case. In fact, at one point, we believed our child's life was ruined because of the impact a failed semester of high school would have on his college applications.

Despite earning great grades and having an all-around fantastic sophomore year in high school, at the end of his first semester of his junior year, we learned that our son had failed all his courses, and he was ready to drop out altogether. In fact, he did end up dropping out a month later.

Our son has a magnetic personality and is usually an excellent student. Even a year prior, we could imagine his high school trajectory with the opposite ending: filled with many academic, leadership, and extracurricular accolades. But instead, in a change that happened over a matter of months, his high school narrative transformed from bright and successful to dim and failing. It's not an overstatement to say that we felt that because of this, his life was ruined. Our beautiful boy with such a bright future! And now—all that potential, all that promise—dashed! Squandered! Thrown away! Lost forever! What college could he go to now? Could he even get into any college? What jobs would he ever be able to get? What quality of life could he ever hope to have?!

We invite you to mentally transport yourself in time and space to sit in this moment with us and feel our fear and anxiety upon learning that not only had our son's high school record been ruined, he'd dropped out entirely. A child dropping out of high school is cause for concern.

We (Americans) have very specific ideas of what a successful high school student looks like: excelling academically and in extracurricular activities. The two of us had hewed closely to these expectations in our own high school careers and knew cautionary tales of folks who hadn't. And our son was looking like a cautionary tale. At the time, it was unthinkable that his college applications could overcome what looked like an obvious failure. Getting into college is complicated and competitive enough, even with a consistently stellar high school experience. Adding the deadweight of a failed semester and dropping out seemed insurmountable at the time.

Thankfully, we couldn't have been more wrong.

For the purposes of this book, the details of why he dropped out aren't important. In retrospect, it was largely due to complications in communications between a French high school and an American high school, and our failure as parents to adequately monitor his academics the first semester of his junior year of high school, when he was studying abroad. But the lessons we learned aren't limited to parents with students who struggle because of a semester abroad. The result would be the same if our child had dropped out because he fell into a "bad" group of friends, or had experienced a debilitating bout of depression, or got into trouble with the law. We can empathize with parents who feel that all hope is lost for a child who struggles or drops out of school, and we are much more confident speaking about great options for such children.

As parents, we were distraught, worried that we had squandered his potential by first choosing to disrupt his US schooling by moving to France and not moving back in time for his freshman year to make sure he had a straightforward high school transcript as was the original plan. He was the type of child who earned straight As during a typical school year. He was an all-star student, whom teachers loved to have in class, and he made friends easily. He seemed like he was on track to become student body president. In terms of our missteps, we had taken our son's gold and spun it into straw.

After his failed semester, and before he dropped out of school, our first instinct was to do everything we could to get him back onto the path he had been on: Go to summer school to retake the courses he had failed, get excellent grades for the remaining semesters, and then apply to a great college. In rationalizing the path forward, we reasoned that what he had lost was any flexibility or leeway for the remaining semesters—so school would need to be really intense from now on. But to complicate things further, he was also just feeling *done* with high school. He felt like he had experienced everything he wanted to experience as a high school student and wanted to move on to the next thing. To him, buckling down on high school even more felt like a step backward.

We had several weeks of soul searching, and when we were really feeling at a loss, a friend recommended we speak with a college entrance counselor who had experience working with "complicated" high school records. We made an appointment for an initial consultation, and we were prepared for the worst. That conversation with the counselor switched something for us. The counselor confirmed our fears that our son's high school transcript would need to be repaired or he wouldn't be able to get into a university, and we all wanted him to have a good university experience. He suggested three options:

1) Our son could go to summer school and fix his bad grades from his failed semester. Barring that, he could work to ace the SAT, and take as many AP courses as possible independently. This would demonstrate his academic proficiency and give him a narrative of a solid high school transcript with one out-of-the-ordinary failing semester.

2) He could transfer to a private school and work with the counselor at that school to translate his experiences into high school credits, or into a narrative report card. He suggested that private schools often have more flexibility in these areas than public schools and could essentially rebuild his transcript based on new work.

3) He could take the GED, be done with high school, and enroll at a community college, then transfer to a good university after two years.

Option one was our initial first choice. It would take a lot of intense work—he would not have a summer break and would basically have to get perfect grades for the next year and a half, while taking a lot of demanding courses. And he would need to prepare to ace the SAT. Option two would also be intense, plus it would cost a lot—in the neighborhood of thirty thousand dollars per year for tuition, and we weren't in a position to afford that. Option three was the least intense— it would involve preparation for the GED, but that was manageable, and he wouldn't need to ace it, just pass it. No AP courses required; no SAT prep required. He would be finished with high school immediately.

After discussing the options with our son, we hesitatingly chose option three. We are embarrassed to say that we had been taught to disdain community college to some degree, viewing it as something to be a bit ashamed about. There was also the worry that he wouldn't be able to transfer to a four-year university, or whether he would even want to when the time came—one concern the counselor mentioned is that the percentage of community college students who actually transfer is small.

Readers who are familiar with community college will know how wrong we were. One of the key roles of community college is to provide a bridge from high school to college, especially for students who didn't excel in high school, or for whatever reason were not ready or willing to jump into a four-year program straight out of high school. So our son signed up for the next scheduled GED test (in California, the GED is called the CHSPE), studied for it, and passed it easily. He was done with high school and on a new path.

Here's how his college path played out: He enrolled in community college classes at Berkeley City College (a community college near Berkeley University). In California, there is a program that guarantees acceptance to the prestigious UC school system if a student takes a specific series of community college classes and receives good grades. We attended a meeting with our son and his campus counselor to make sure we knew exactly which classes he needed to take to qualify for this program.

He excelled in his classes and appreciated the range of ages and experience among his fellow students. After a semester of classes, our son decided to go on a church mission and was assigned to go to Bogotá, Colombia. He worked in Colombia for two years, and became fluent in Spanish. When he returned, he enrolled again in community college for another year and a half—which was extended by another year because of the pandemic.

Once he completed the required classes for the UC transfer program, he applied and was accepted to UC Berkeley. At first, he was hesitant about doing more college, and wondered if it was worth investing more time and energy toward a degree. But he was offered a full scholarship and decided to go for it. It turns out he *loved* attending Cal. With the two-year mission and the pandemic break, he was a bit older than some of his fellow students, but he was also much more enthusiastic than he would have been at eighteen. He loved studying; he loved writing essays; he loved the whole concept of a liberal arts education—he wanted *everyone* to get a chance to learn to think critically and read widely and write papers and discuss everything they were learning.

All that worry as parents, and yet, our son ended up graduating from UC Berkeley with top grades and a full scholarship, without taking the SAT, or worrying about AP tests, or a superstressful junior and senior high school year, or overwhelming college applications. And he enjoyed all sorts of adventures along the way, coming away with a great academic experience and a newfound appreciation for the offerings of a college education.

Now our more educated response to the experience of a child dropping out of high school is that parents should not lose hope. Community colleges are typically significantly less expensive than a four-year university—so completing half of your college credits through community college can cut the cost of college nearly in half. Community colleges also don't have complicated applications. And community colleges often offer open enrollment, meaning anyone with a high school diploma or equivalent (like completing the GED) can enroll.

Enrolling in a four-year university immediately after graduation from high school is a great option for some students, especially if the child is prepared, and the cost is manageable. But this is not the only option. In addition to community college, there are trade schools, coding schools, and professional licensing organizations, and we believe that these options* will only improve and increase in the future.

---

* Ben's career is a bet on alternatives to "the reliable path to success" and on the changing face of higher education. Ben is the cofounder and president of Newlane University (newlane.edu), an online university that offers truly affordable accredited bachelor's degrees. Newlane is part of a growing wave of education initiatives looking to make quality higher education more affordable and more accessible to a wider range of people.

A college education is still—deservedly—an important and valuable marker in American society, and will continue to be for the foreseeable future. But this doesn't mean that the high cost of a college degree is justified, or that the anxiety and stress parents and their kids shoulder to get into a four-year university are warranted. Our recommendation is to help your child aim for college if that path makes the most sense, but don't feel like you must stick to the path at all costs. As we've seen up close, there are so many paths with positive outcomes, and so many chances to start over with a clean slate and try again.

WHY YOU DON'T NEED TO WORRY ABOUT YOUR CHILD'S FUTURE CAREER

In 2010, Gabrielle was four years into the blogging portion of her career (she had started her blog, *Design Mom*, in 2006). The year 2010 was the heyday of blogging, and *Time* named *Design Mom* a Parenting Website of the Year. *Design Mom* was one of a handful of sites the magazine honored with this title—and it even used the logo Gabrielle had designed for her blog as the visual for the whole article. It was Gabrielle's first major acknowledgment from traditional media, and it felt amazing. Her friends in the blogging community celebrated the news. We lived in Colorado at the time, and when Gabrielle woke up, the news had already spread among her friends on the East Coast. When she started her workday, she learned about the *Time* designation from dozens of tweets. The blogging community was so excited—like, *wow!*—one of their own had been acknowledged by an influential publication. It was a big deal.

A few months later, Gabrielle was giving a talk at a conference for bloggers (yes, there were conferences back then specifically for bloggers). During the talk Gabrielle shared some slides featuring charts and numbers showing how much traffic her blog had received from *Time* since *Design Mom* was named one of its Parenting Websites of the Year. And it was a lot of traffic. And then Gabrielle showed another slide showing how much traffic *Design Mom* had received from her sister's midsize lifestyle blog in the same time frame. And it was *ten times as much traffic*. The audience at the conference gasped.

Gabrielle's intention was to demonstrate how influential new media—like the blogs of all the attendees at the conference—could be. Of course, she was really pleased about *Time*'s acknowledgment, but what, she asked, was the real point of being featured in legacy media? For Gabrielle, the biggest value wasn't traffic—it was that her mom now had a way to explain to friends and others in her community what her daughter did for a living. She could say, "You know *Time*? Well, they called Gabrielle's website a top website of the year." It gave instant credibility, an easy-to-understand credential. Before that, Gabrielle's mother would tell people that Gabrielle was a blogger, which meant nothing to her mom's peers—the words *blog* and *blogger* and *blogging* were still relatively new, and it all sounded sort of pretend or silly. But Gabrielle's mom was proud of her and having this recognizable honor from *Time* made it seem more real and easier to talk about.

Since 2010, the number of parents who don't understand or can't describe what their adult children do for work has only increased. Jobs are different now.

Maybe you have a job that is easy to describe. You're a doctor or a lawyer or an accountant or a shopkeeper. When we were growing up, our generation assumed we would all have those types of jobs, jobs we'd heard of and understood. Ben studied to be a college professor. Gabrielle studied to be a graphic designer. And those were our jobs when we first finished school.

But now, we both have jobs that didn't exist when we were in school, that didn't really exist even a decade ago. We don't even know what to call Gabrielle's current job. Content creator? Blogger? Renovation influencer? Twitter essayist? And Ben's job title is currently a university president. Yes, that's the type of job (and title) that is actually pretty old-school— but in Ben's case, the university is a school he created himself (together with his cofounder), from scratch, with technology that didn't exist until a few years ago.

There are a whole lot of jobs that exist now that didn't exist just a few years ago. And there are jobs that have been around seemingly forever that are now disappearing. It makes it a lot harder to talk to our kids about their future.

It's one thing if your child tells you they want to be a lawyer because it's a concrete professional goal that can be accomplished with specific, established steps. *We can help with that! Here's an LSAT study guide!* But if your child tells you they want to be a Twitch streamer and play *Minecraft*, you might think: *Is that a real thing? Is it something lots of people can do for a living? Or is it accessible to only a few Twitch celebrities? Is there a college major for this? A book we should read? How do we help you achieve this goal?*

Because we lived through it, we can draw a line from our past to our present careers. But the mistake is to believe we can likewise draw the line from the present to the future, and that if our kids just do what we did, they'll have the same opportunities and results.

It's 2024 as we write this book. Twenty years ago, in 2004, Gabrielle was a senior art director at an advertising agency in New York. She worked in a skyscraper with offices and cubicles. She did graphic design, and her job was easy to describe. This was the job she thought she would have when she majored in graphic design in college.

In 2006, she started *Design Mom*, an entirely different career. She was a blogger. She learned to write well. She learned photography. She worked from home and tried to figure out how to make money from being a blogger—selling ads in the margins, then later doing sponsored blog posts. Facebook was soon at its peak and pushed bloggers to video. Now Gabrielle was making and editing videos. Then Instagram became the most influential social media platform, and blogging began to fade. Now she had to master Instagram, including Instagram Stories—a totally new format. She started and ran a conference, learning how to host and organize in-person events. She launched a subscription newsletter. She learned to write books and make book proposals, and how to promote books too.

Twenty years later, and guess what's not really a career anymore? Blogging. Back in 2006, Gabrielle had to learn and build a whole new career from scratch, but now her workday looks entirely different than it did when she started blogging. She's had six or seven distinct jobs since then. That's how fast the world is changing. In 2024, a parent might think, *I should get my child into AI development because that's the future*. But that would be like telling your child in 2008 that they need to get good at blogging because blogging is the future.

It's not just blogging/content creator/influencer work that is changing quickly. Journalism hasn't disappeared (thank goodness) but getting a job in journalism isn't something you can depend on like you could twenty or thirty years ago. Writing legal briefs is predicted to become a job for AI; so is reading X-rays. Even five years ago, someone might have said, "Well, if you're a software engineer, you will always have a job." But that's not true anymore. Careers that we assumed would always be there aren't as stable as we thought they were. There is no silver bullet for the future.

It's not just specific jobs that are changing, the entire nature of work is changing. How we think about work is changing—from assuming we'll be working in an office building to demanding that we can work from home instead. We've seen that shift just in the last few years. Will flexible schedules become a common feature of work life, or will they fade away? We don't know.

There are ongoing conversations about universal basic income (UBI) and about establishing a four-day workweek as the norm. There are conversations about care work and how people should be compensated for caring for aging parents and young children (instead of assuming women will do this work for free).

It used to be you would get a job, and you would stick with that for forty years. Now, changing careers several times throughout a lifetime is commonplace. And there are predictions that our children won't work at all—or at least won't "work" in a way that we recognize as a job.

This is why we don't worry about our kids' future professional lives. We can't control how fast the world is changing. We can't control what jobs will be available for our kids.

So this is what we do instead: We try to make sure our kids get a good education, that they're flexible and independent, and that they're not afraid of hard work. And then we trust that their flexibility and their independence mean they're going to figure things out. From what we've observed, the professional trends are moving toward individuals being able to find or create work that provides value to others and that they are passionate about, instead of being mostly limited to finding and taking established pathways to specific, recognizable jobs. And that hasn't been the case for most people for most of history. So that's good news.

We encourage our kids to embrace lifelong learning. If they have specialties that they really like—maybe math or history or *D&D*—then we lean into those. We encourage them to pursue those interests even if we don't know what they'll do with them for a career or if they'll use them in their career at all. Maybe they'll teach their interest, maybe they'll end up in a traditional job, or maybe they'll end up with a job (or create a job) that didn't exist before.

We try to avoid the instinct to put all their eggs in one basket or set up expectations for a specific outcome. Even if they take all the established steps toward a specific career goal, careers are no longer guaranteed.

We look for opportunities where our kids can be exposed to lots of different work experiences: Volunteer at a soup kitchen or as a student helper in the cafeteria. Try a summer internship while they still live at home and don't have expenses. Have them shadow one of your friends at work for the day. Take a tour of a tech company campus. Help out at a friend's small business. Host a career night for neighborhood families where the adults talk about what they do for work. Point out the jobs of the grown-ups they know. Point out the wide variety of jobs they encounter as you run errands. Help them understand that jobs will continue to change, and there are a million ways to work.

2

STAYING FLEXIBLE AND OPEN TO CHANGE

WHY WE REMIND OURSELVES OUR CHILD IS NOT US, AND OUR CHILDHOOD IS NOT THEIR CHILDHOOD

One weekend, when our daughter was fifteen, she and Ben were watching a football game on TV. Ben realized for the first time that this daughter didn't know the basics of football. So, he began explaining (dad-splaining?) the rules of the game. Her response? "Why would I need to know the rules of football? When would this be useful?" Ben was dumbfounded that anyone—much less his child—could be so uninterested in football, and so oblivious to the significance of the game. Ben explained that knowing the rules of football is important cultural knowledge to have. It certainly was for us during our childhoods.

Ben remembers fall Saturdays were usually built around the BYU football game. His dad had season tickets for home games, and most away games were televised, so a good part of each Saturday from September to January was devoted to watching the game either in person or on TV. Football was a vital and treasured part of his childhood. For Gabrielle, too, much of her high school social scene revolved around football games, and the dances that happened afterward. Football seemed like an essential part of life in both our towns. Football also made for easy talking points and shared experiences with parents, neighbors, classmates, cousins, and Grandpa and Grandma. A victory could transform a miserable, cold Saturday into a day of celebration. A loss could transform the perfect fall weekend into one of despair.

Before we had kids, if you had asked either of us what the chances were that any of our children would not know the basic rules of football, we both would have said 0 percent. And yet here we are twenty-seven years later, and most of our six kids couldn't name an NFL team and don't have even a basic understanding of how downs work. Most of our kids didn't attend high schools where there was a football game every Friday night in the fall. Their PE curriculums didn't include football. They didn't grow up in a university town with a popular football team. We never owned season tickets for any team.

Sadly, this means that our children haven't experienced the communal thrill of defeating a rival school or (happily) the gut punch of a bungled lead. They haven't reveled with classmates and family about an amazing play or victory. Outside of the occasional Super Bowl (which has become as much a holiday as a football game), we rarely watch any football in our home. This activity that was so vital and pervasive for us growing up was effectively nonexistent for our children.

Our child is not us, and our childhood is not their childhood.

In 2009, we moved to Colorado from New York, where we had lived since 2001, and where three of our (then) five children had been born. This move was emotional for the whole family. Saying goodbye to good friends and a strong community with no plan to ever return was incredibly hard. We were venturing into a scary unknown, and all felt a mixture of excitement and apprehension about this new adventure—our children had only ever known what it was like to live in New York, and none of us had ever lived in Colorado.

We both grew up in Utah in different towns that were four hours apart (Provo and St. George). From the age of five to adulthood, we each lived in our own same towns in our same neighborhoods, on our same streets, and in our same houses. There was a comforting consistency to this life. From Ben's earliest memory, the sound of his neighbor's snowblower clearing the sidewalks heralded every snowy morning like clockwork, and Gabrielle could expect summer downpours that dotted and quenched the very hot desert landscape. Each of us, in our own towns, frequented the same grocery stores, barber shops, doctors, dentists, and restaurants growing up. Our geography was fixed: To get oriented anywhere in the world, Ben still imagines Mount Timpanogos for the North, and Gabrielle still imagines the Red Hill for the West.

Growing up this way was wonderful—no one has to convince us of the value of deep roots. Our childhood environments are within us at what feels like a cellular level, and even decades later, these ultrafamiliar environments are the "normal" against which every new place or new experience is measured and assessed.

Our move from New York confronted us with the reality that if we wanted our children to have the same familiar setting throughout their childhood that we had both experienced, the only possibility would be to stay in New York. And we were choosing against that.

Our child is not us, and our childhood is not their childhood.

"How you make sense of your childhood experiences has a profound effect on how you parent your own children." This is how psychologists Daniel J. Siegel and Mary Hartzel open their landmark book *Parenting from the Inside Out*.

We would add that our childhood experiences have a profound effect on how we parent whether or not we've ever made sense of them, or even tried to make sense of them. Whether we know it or not, our childhood experiences often serve as a template or model for how we parent, whether we want to repeat history—or reject it.

Maybe as a child you always wished you could take ice-skating lessons, but you never got the chance, so you sign up your child at the local rink as soon as they can fit into skates. Maybe your own parents were not affectionate, so you shower your kids with hugs and kisses. Maybe you loved growing up on a cul-de-sac and playing night games with other kids in the neighborhood, so you prioritize finding a house on a cul-de-sac for your own kids to grow up in. Maybe you loved the holidays as a child and want them to be magical for your own kids so you put in lots of time and effort to make that happen.

But despite our best intentions, we can't predict what these choices will mean for our kids. Our children might appreciate these decisions. They might be neutral on these decisions. They also might hate these decisions. The house on the cul-de-sac may seem like a bummer of a location to your teen who has zero interest in learning to drive and wishes your house was superclose to a public transit hub. Staying too close to a path that feels familiar can keep us stuck in something that isn't really working for us, or for our kids.

As young parents, we decided that we couldn't let the things we loved about our past dictate how we would live with the family we were building.

Ben doesn't push football with any of our kids, and our children have not had a childhood marked by a consistent cast of characters, home, or town. There is unquestionably a loss to this. But it isn't *only* a loss. Our children have also had experiences we never had at their age, like learning another language, participating in orchestra, and doing a pilgrimage.

Maybe this has been easier for us to appreciate since our children's childhoods are so markedly different from ours, but even if we had raised our kids in the same towns, same houses, and same streets where we grew up, and their weekends were devoted to football games, that still wouldn't have delivered the same experience.

Understanding that your child is not you and that their childhood is not your childhood can feel strange. Some of the most stressful times we've experienced as parents have been when we went off the script that we were raised on. And we don't think we're alone in this.

In some cases, the difference between you and your child is small, like not liking football or not liking chocolate. In some cases, it's a little bigger, like growing up in a different country and culture than the one you grew up in. And in some cases, the differences can feel vast, such as a child who rejects your religion, or other ways of life and traditions that are important to you.

Of course, some of the most satisfying parenting moments are when we see the pleasures of our own childhoods reflected in our children—when they run for student government, or gleefully jump into swimming holes. It's gratifying to see the things that meant so much to us mean something to our kids. It can feel like time travel—a way to revisit our past selves. It can feel like connection—bonding over shared childhood experiences. It can feel like a gift we've given our kids—passing along the things that meant something to us, and seeing it mean something to them.

But in our experience, understanding that our kids are not us, and that our childhoods are not their childhoods, has forced us to question why we prioritized certain activities, like sports, music lessons, or academics, and how we responded when our children resisted our advice. And it has meant more open-ended conversations with our children about their desires, aspirations, and fears. We've learned to prioritize listening and trust. In learning to ride out those moments of disconnect, we've found that they are, counterintuitively, opportunities for deep connection. Our children can feel seen and supported and trusted—and we feel emboldened to take our own risks without fear that one false step will mean disaster.

A lot of stress and anxiety falls away when we accept that we are parenting the children we have, not the children we were, not the children we anticipated, and not the children we imagined. And that we're parenting them in the world as it exists today.

WHY FLEXIBILITY IS KEY

There are two systemic issues

that we spent a dozen really challenging years trying to resolve: the cultural expectation of rigid work schedules, and the cultural expectation of raising children in isolation.

When we finally did find workarounds, parenting became significantly more manageable. And we think the same could be true for you.

Let's talk about rigid work schedules first, because we've seen some hopeful improvement on this issue over the last several years. This is obvious, but the solution to fixing the stress that rigid work schedules bring is making flexible work schedules the norm instead. Many of us saw this happen during pandemic lockdowns where any job that could be done at home was transformed instantly into a remote position.

For us, this wasn't new—we'd had remote, flexible work schedules for a decade already. We started down this flexible schedule road early on in our marriage (we've been married for twenty-nine years as of this writing). This was when the internet was still quite new and remote work wasn't really a thing. Ben was building language programs at local schools, and Gabrielle had her design clients, and we couldn't afford childcare, so we started splitting the workdays. Gabrielle would work from 8:00 a.m. to 12:00 p.m. while Ben did the parenting, then we would have lunch all together, and then Ben would work from 1:00 p.m. to 5:00 p.m. while Gabrielle did the parenting. We tried to work as efficiently as possible and pack an entire workday into those four hours (somewhat doable since we didn't have office interruptions or a lot of meetings), but we also fit in additional work in the evenings after the kids had gone to bed. That was our first effort at sharing both the work and parenting loads, and it improved our lives by a mile.

Then we moved to New York for graduate school, and we had to find a different balance. We took it year by year, semester by semester, and generally took turns working full-time while the other person was the primary parent. We still couldn't afford more than a few hours a week of childcare, so we had to get creative. At one point, we traded room and board for childcare. A friend moved in with us who had an internship in the city two days per week, and on the other days she helped us with the kids, so Ben could attend his classes. We made it work, adapting our schedules every few months as needed, but we missed splitting our workdays like we had previously and wished we could do something like that again.

By the end of our time in New York, after an assortment of full-time jobs and freelance and adjunct work, we had come up with a pretty great situation. Gabrielle had started a blog, *Design Mom*, and that had led to more online design work and online writing. Ben had finished his PhD and was working full-time for an education company in Washington, DC, that allowed Ben to work from home in New York.

Suddenly, after nearly a dozen years of juggling our work and parenting responsibilities, we both had full-time work from home, which meant for the first time ever we both had totally flexible work schedules. It was amazing—even more amazing than when we used to split our workdays—and it changed everything for us.

A few months into this new situation, we moved to Colorado and put our flexible schedules to use. Gabrielle continued daily work on *Design Mom* and also started a conference with her sister. (The conference is called Alt Summit, and it's for people like Gabrielle—creative professionals and entrepreneurs who work online.) Ben continued his remote position in curriculum development and expanded into evaluating other online schools and programs. And then: We had another baby. Baby number six!

It meant a world of difference that we could both work from home and could control our work hours. We had all these little kids and challenging work projects, and a busy home to run, but we could make it all happen because we never had to get permission to take a half day off for a doctor visit for the kids, or to go volunteer in the classroom, or to see the Halloween costume parade. If the kids were sick, we didn't need to arrange childcare. We still hired babysitters from time to time if we were especially busy, or for date nights, but we didn't need help full-time.

Once we had experienced it, having a flexible schedule seemed nonnegotiable for those years when we had babies and toddlers and preschoolers, but it also made parenting much easier during the school-age years. Maybe you want to be an involved parent, you want to go read to your child's class, or participate in their school career-day presentation. If you don't have a flexible work schedule, you have to plan far ahead and arrange to get off work for the morning. And if you didn't know about the volunteer classroom opportunity until the last minute, you may be out of luck, because you didn't talk to your boss ahead of time.

And maybe you need to be at school for only an hour—say from 11:00 a.m. to 12 p.m.—but you end up missing five hours of work, because it's not worth commuting in and then turning around immediately, and then coming back again. So that feels like a waste. And if you're paid by the hour, it *is* a waste. And you end up feeling like you're missing out on parenting moments that you don't want to miss out on. That can be really, really frustrating.

Being a parent and not having a flexible work schedule makes it especially clear how our entire parenting culture is built around the assumption that every parent is married, and that in every married couple, one parent will be home full-time—which is especially maddening because we know that's actually pretty rare. There are appointments and errands that must be done that are possible only during standard work hours. When is a working parent supposed to go to those appointments and run those errands? And the school schedule makes it obvious as well. Kids often get out of school at 3:00 p.m., some kindergarten programs are only a half day, and school lets out for the summer break for eight to ten weeks. Who is supposed to be caring for the kids during work hours if there's not a stay-at-home parent? And if there is a stay-at-home parent, while it can help the childcare situation, it can also bring up other hard issues—like lack of income, a major parenting imbalance, and a harmful break in work history; for some, it's a cause of depression.

This leads us to that second systemic issue: the cultural expectation of raising kids in isolation. Years ago, during Gabrielle's full-time stay-at-home experience, when we had two kids, Gabrielle learned a lesson that stuck with us. She was in the middle of a diaper change for the baby (who was just a few weeks old) when she heard the toddler (who was just one and a half) scream in pain. She couldn't leave the baby on the changing table, so she picked her up without finishing the diaper change, to go find the toddler. He was a few steps away in the kitchen of our small apartment and had hit his head on the corner of a lower cupboard door. His forehead was gushing blood. This was the first bleeding accident Gabrielle had faced as a mother and she was terrified. She put the baby down while she attended to the bleeding toddler. The baby, who was still mid–diaper change, was very upset at being set down and started screaming. The toddler, in pain from the gash on his forehead, was also crying hard. Gabrielle was able to get the bleeding to stop, but the gash looked deep, and she wanted to go see our pediatrician right away, in case the toddler needed stitches. All three—Gabrielle, toddler, and baby—were a mess, covered in blood and baby poop; all three were crying, and the baby still needed to be fed. Gabrielle got everyone calmed down and cleaned up enough to get out the door, buckled into car seats, and headed off to the doctor's office. She was sad and worried as they drove off, but by the time they got to the doctor's office, she was *furious*. She wondered: *Why was there only one adult at home?! Why do we isolate mothers like this? It makes parenting much harder than it needs to be! It's not practical and it makes no sense!*

Picture the challenges of a parent doing care work in isolation, and then imagine how quickly things would improve if there were multiple adults around. Multiple adults at home doing care work means they get turns to rest and don't fall asleep leaving the babies unattended. It means they get breaks in their workday, they get adult conversation, they can more easily handle emergencies, they can separate a sick kid from a healthy kid to prevent spreading illness. Having multiple caregivers around means there's less chance of losing patience with kids who need attention and less chance of responding in anger. It means no one needs to hold the baby while stirring at a hot stove and risking a burn.

It's frustrating and bizarre that our culture sets us up to parent in isolation. It would make far more sense to be raising our babies with help from siblings, aunts and uncles, parents and grandparents, neighbors and friends. Raising kids is difficult work, and our culture makes it far harder than it needs to be by insisting we do it alone.

Honestly, we never found the ideal fix for this issue; we didn't find an equivalent to the flexible work schedule and start raising our kids with a whole team of committed caregivers. But we did get a taste of what it looks like to not parent in isolation.

Coming up with solutions (or partial solutions) for these two systemic problems changed everything for us. So many of those very real stresses and concerns were resolved because we had two committed caregivers at home and flexible work schedules, so we could both fit our paid work around our parenting work.

We recognize that not all work can be done remotely, but if you'd like a flexible work schedule, start making moves toward that right away. It took us years, but eventually we did get there. If you already have the kind of work that *can* be done remotely, fight for that. Fight for full-time remote work. If you can't get that, fight for remote work on one or two days each week—it will still make a huge difference. Even being able to choose last-minute remote work two or three days each *month* would still allow you to accommodate sick kids, or a surprise doctor visit, or an impromptu school outing. In our experience, a flexible work schedule affects the experience of parenting more than probably anything else, so it's a worthwhile goal to aim for. It's okay to want these things. Parents *deserve* these things!

You're not a failure if you want help as a parent, or if you want a work schedule that accommodates parenting. Those are not unreasonable things to want. What's unreasonable is that we've been conditioned to think that these hopes or expectations reflect a personal weakness instead of a systemic issue.

And once your kids are older—like when they're in high school—the needs change. Having a more rigid work schedule at that time may be much more doable.

For those who don't have another caregiver (or multiple caregivers) in their household to help with parenting, building a community becomes even more crucial. It may take a lot of time and effort to realize, but it can make a profound difference. Can you live near parents or siblings or close friends—people you can rely on when you need an extra set of hands? Can you build a network of neighbors or fellow parents from your child's school? Picture the "pods" during the Covid shutdowns—multiple families who shared some of the schooling and parenting burdens. Could you form a parenting pod of sorts with other parents who have flexible schedules and share some of the parenting responsibilities among the group?

Ultimately, if a flexible schedule or shared caregiving are what you want, then work toward that. And if you see a family that seems to have it all together, assume they've found workarounds for these two systemic problems.

We're going to end this discussion by bringing up one more factor affecting both of these systemic issues: money. If you are wealthy, you can make workarounds for these issues quite easily. If you need additional caregivers to assist you, you can simply hire them. If you want a more flexible work schedule, you have the resources and security to negotiate that or find another position (or retire early!).

The other money-related part of this discussion is our selective obliviousness about the value a parent provides to the community by raising a child. Our culture and economy absolutely depend on parenting and caregiving work but refuse to compensate it. It's really high-value labor, but it's largely unpaid and unrecognized. This work is typically done by women, and our entire economy is built on the expectation that women will continue to do this unpaid work.

If our economy could figure out a way to compensate for this work accurately and fairly, that would also go a long way in solving these two systemic issues. We're not holding our breath for this to happen in the very near future, but there is an increasing awareness of the costs of childcare, and a growing grassroots movement around the idea of compensating parents or providing a universal basic income to all adults. We believe there are reasons for cautious optimism and something worthwhile to work toward.

HOW TO MAKE FAMILY BONDS THAT LAST

In 2009 we moved from New York to Colorado with the intention to permanently settle. Ben's sister found us a good rental house that was significantly less expensive than what we were paying in New York so we could save up to buy a home. After the first year, we welcomed our last child, and started looking in earnest for our permanent home.

We explored some great neighborhoods with beautiful mid-century modern architecture. We looked in nearby neighborhoods and others closer to the mountains. We spoke with a Realtor and also asked our landlords whether they were interested in selling. We had a good idea of what we were looking for: an older home, with a certain architectural profile that seemed common enough, but also with enough rooms for our family. We spent many weekends looking at houses within an hour of our rental home and returned to some neighborhoods multiple times.

We came close to making an offer on several houses, but they either didn't fit our budget, or didn't meet some important criteria. We spoke with friends and a Realtor about this dilemma, hoping they might know of other places to look— but they suggested that if we were set on those characteristics, patience was the strategy.

In retrospect, it was an odd sort of calculus to make, but rather than continue to patiently look for houses to purchase from the comfort of our rental, we started to contemplate a different adventure. The thinking was something like this: If it is going to take more time to find a home than we had planned, rather than bide that time, we could spend it by trying something different. After all, the market for rentals like the one we were living in was reliable, and we could always come back to something similar. We reasoned we could also continue to research the real estate market from wherever we were, and if our dream house came up, we could still jump on it.

We always wanted to live abroad and it's something we talked a lot about with our kids. When Ben was a freshman in college, he moved to Russia and lived with a Russian family, teaching English to their four-year-old. In our second year of marriage, while we were expecting our first child, we moved to Athens, Greece, for a research project on the Greek school system (Ben) and an advertising agency internship (Gabrielle). Our children's aunts and uncles and grandparents had lived and worked or served missions for extended periods in Japan, Brazil, Colombia, Ecuador, Cambodia, Russia, Germany, China, Guatemala, Taiwan, and more. Ben's father was a linguist who spoke a number of languages—he kept us stocked with language courses. Our kids grew up knowing that moving abroad could always be a possibility.

While not every family can seriously entertain a move abroad, and not every family would want to, we found the idea endlessly appealing. We recognize it's a privilege to be able to consider moving abroad—your income must be stable enough to qualify for a residence visa, and your employer must be flexible enough to allow remote work. We could not have contemplated such a move if either of our jobs required in-person office attendance.

For us, it felt like an ideal time to try something new and different. Our oldest child was starting seventh grade and it seemed to us that if we spent one year abroad, missing the second half of seventh and the first half of eighth grade would be only a minor disruption to his schooling, and the disruptions for the younger kids would be smaller still. The best time for someone to learn a foreign language is when they are young, so the timing would never get better. And maybe it was partially a coping mechanism for not being able to find a house, but it was really easy to get excited about a new adventure. We couldn't justify the costs of an international vacation with a family of eight. But the difference between an international vacation and a move abroad is that the vacation expenses are on top of the expenses of your regular life—you still pay your regular rent on top of the flight, car rental, and hotel. A move abroad still includes travel, but swaps one rent and car payment, etc., for another.

We were only going to go for one year. Our goal was an adventure for our family—let them see a little more of the world and learn a language and experience another culture.

And that's really it. We were exchanging a status quo year in the same place with frequent disappointments about not finding our permanent home for an exciting and adventurous year abroad! We started by looking for rentals on Craigslist, and found a place in Dieppe, on the northwest coast of France, that seemed interesting, but it wasn't furnished, and we weren't sure how we would manage furnishing a place in a new country.

Gabrielle mentioned the possibility of a move abroad on her blog and someone turned us on to SabbaticalHomes.com, and this site seemed to address just what we were looking for: furnished homes available for extended stays. We entered our criteria, including budget, number of rooms and bathrooms, and distance from Paris, and this funnel resulted in one home—a farmhouse in Normandy, just outside of the town of Argentan. We reached out, and to our delight, the owner was an Australian and French couple, so there was no language barrier either (we could only speak a little French).

The home was about the same rent we were paying in Colorado (sometimes slightly more, sometimes slightly less, depending on the dollar-euro exchange rate). It was a stunning property in the Normandy countryside, with neighboring small family farms to buy eggs or milk, bikes for idyllic country rides, a spacious backyard, a picturesque tree house, wall paneling repurposed from a chateau, gorgeous stone floors in the kitchen from the 1700s, a large art studio, big gathering rooms for the whole family, and every surface of the home painstakingly beautified by the amazing artist/craftsman owner-landlord.

Because we had imagined only one year abroad, we were going to enroll the children in online school—this would ensure they didn't fall behind and would also allow more flexibility for our family for this one year. However, our children are very social, and within a few days in our new farmhouse, the kids wanted to see what the local school might be like. So we enrolled them in school, reasoning that we could withdraw them after a week if it wasn't working.

None of us could have guessed how difficult school would be. Partly this was because there was no French-as-a-second-language program, and no significant support for international students, so our children were dropped in and immediately were the worst students in the class (except in English, of course). The French school culture was also totally different than in the United States—probably the biggest difference was the practice of reading grades aloud in class, and the fact that public shaming of students by teachers is a normalized part of the school day. In fact, as our kids began to learn French and started rising from the lowest score in the class, the students who did worse than our kids would often hear, "Even the *American* did better than you!"

Our kids would return home from school exhausted from eight hours of trying to understand what sounded like gibberish to their ears. Progress was slow. It was really hard, and we don't want to downplay that. Yet our kids had no desire to stop—they were making friends, making progress in French, and enjoying their school experience despite the challenges. A two-hour lunch break, with a daily three-course meal served by the school, certainly helped. We told our kids that we didn't care about their grades, and that their primary job was to learn to speak French and to learn about French school culture, which meant they weren't burdened by report cards. And our kids didn't feel alone in their challenges; they were sharing this experience with their siblings and had one another to commiserate with on the hard days.

But even with that difficult and unrelenting language barrier, which was the hardest part, we loved our life in Normandy. Part of it was that we were in the countryside and a ten-minute drive from town, so we were kind of stuck with one another. And even the difficult language barrier became this unique and intimate shared experience among the children in a way that could recast the difficulty into something they were doing with their siblings. And while school was intense, the kids had two-week breaks every six weeks or so, which meant we could drive to explore other parts of France and Europe and still get in our working hours thanks to our flexible work schedules.

It took some time to find our footing, but once we got acclimated to this slower pace of life, we really embraced living in Normandy. We got to know our neighbors, we made regular visits to the farmers market and bakeries, we got to know members of our church congregation, we started doing language exchanges and tried to get involved—Ben was asked to speak at a local Rotary Club meeting about US elections, and we hosted a huge Easter egg hunt for all our kids' classmates. We made friends with our landlord's family. The kids started doing music, dance, and tennis lessons.

We noticed and embraced the cultural quirks and differences of living abroad. In Normandy, that meant things like: restaurants held strange hours, grocery stores weren't open after 7:00 p.m., and those grocery stores didn't stock familiar

American ingredients, so we had to find new favorite recipes that took advantage of what was available.

We tried to embrace our international experience, knowing that the window for this French adventure was only one year. But as we got close to the end of that year, the kids were feeling more confident at school and had made good friends, and we had all grown to treasure this different life we couldn't have imagined before, so we decided to extend the trip another year.

And then after two years, we extended our stay another six months so our kids could complete their current school year. And by then, they felt quite at ease in French. The experience of school transformed from a strange and indecipherable environment to a place they felt at home, even if they always felt held back to a degree because of the (ever-shrinking) language barrier. We continued to share a lot of family time and scheduled travel excursions during school holidays.

We thought we were getting a break from the stress and disappointment of real estate research. We thought we were getting a one-year interlude before getting back to "real life" in Colorado. We thought we were providing an exciting and prolonged exposure to another language and culture. We left for France identifying as Coloradans on a one-year stint, and returned two and a half years later, not to Colorado, but to a new home in Oakland, California, identifying not as French nor as Coloradan French, but more strongly as a family that now had a changed outlook on the world and ourselves.

Our move to France changed the course of our children's lives and our family's life—it changed our family's narrative.

Not just what our family did and what happened to our family, but how we thought about ourselves and who we were and what we were capable of. It put our kids on a path of future international moves, and learning French fluently opened more opportunities for them. But more fundamental than these opportunities, and maybe a reason for these opportunities, it changed the way all our children view the world, what it means to live somewhere else, what it is like to be a foreigner, the way they view other cultures and languages, how they view themselves, how independent they are, and how open they are for something new and different. A lot of that tracks directly to this first move to Normandy.

So, why are we writing about this? The first lesson isn't that everyone should do a multiyear, transoceanic move. Instead, it's to embrace your life wherever you are—with its quirks, frustrations, and beautiful offerings. The second lesson is to stay open to new possibilities.

The third, and maybe the biggest lesson that we've grown from the most, individually and collectively, is to try new experiences as a family. To take risks together. To have no choice but to trust and rely on one another. Finding our way through a new and strange world forced us to see ourselves in a different light. Our children saw us struggling to communicate in a second language and that removed any illusions of their parents being People Who Know Everything. And we witnessed our children, and they witnessed themselves, working through and overcoming challenges—not just following instructions, but having to do meaningful problem solving in a new-to-them culture and environment. Experiencing this together felt like we were rewiring our family DNA.

We remember being asked for marriage advice, specifically about how we had a strong marriage. And Gabrielle said that one of the most helpful things is that when we were still newly married, just after our first anniversary (at that point, we'd really only known each other for less than two years), we moved somewhere neither of our families had lived or visited (Greece). It was a place where our families had zero ties or connections. We couldn't lean on our parents or siblings or friends. Instead we really had to rely on each other, and determine who we were as a couple without all the noise and influence and pressures of our big families.

Because easy access to email and internet was still new, we couldn't really even talk to our families except for a rare phone call or visit to an internet cafe two hours away. And it bonded us and strengthened our relationship. We came home more confident in each other. We heartily recommended it to every newlywed couple we knew: Move away from both of your families! Even if it's just for six months! And if you can't move away, do something that's unique to just the two of you, something challenging that only the two of you share, something where you won't get feedback or input from family or friends—like restore a car together (as long as no one in your families is a mechanic), or take up a new sport that neither of you have tried before and that no one in your social circles plays.

When our family moved to France—which was another place where our families had no connections—it had the same effect as our move to Greece did as a couple. We had to decide who we were as a family, without the pressures and feedback of grandparents and cousins and friends. We had a chance to figure out our family identity without interference. And it bonded us.

We don't think it's necessary to move to another country to get that bond, but if you do have a move in front of you (across the country or across town), perhaps you can use it to help your family grow closer. And if you don't have a move ahead of you, consider other challenging projects that your family could take on to help forge your family identity and family culture. You can build a playhouse from scratch and learn the building skills together. You can write a book together and self-publish it. You can learn how to rock climb as a family. Look for ideas where everyone in your family is equally a beginner, so that you can all learn and grow together.

3

BUILDING CONNECTION AND FOSTERING INDEPENDENCE

HOW TO BUILD A FAMILY CULTURE WITH INTENTION

"Family culture" is a phrase that can feel big and vague, but ultimately it's pretty straightforward— it's how we interact with one another, what we value, how we spend our time together (and what we choose not to do), and in general, how we, as a family, show up in the world.

Gabrielle started getting a clear picture of her childhood family culture at age eleven. In sixth grade, Gabrielle went to a new-to-her school, where her father was a teacher. Before the first day of school, Gabrielle's mom prepped her. She knew there would be kids (and their parents) who would harass Gabrielle about her dad. He was a big, loud, nonconformist, who wore head-to-toe yellow and was one of about five Democrats in their little town. People had strong opinions about Gabrielle's dad. Her mom told Gabrielle that there were two ways she could respond if anyone said anything mean to her about her dad: 1) Gabrielle could put her thumb on her nose, stretch out her fingers and wiggle them—essentially an eleven-year-old-appropriate hand gesture for *get lost*.

Or, 2)she could say, *Well, you should hear what he says about you!* And then walk away.

Both these suggestions came in handy.

Gabrielle's mom was teaching the lesson that standing up to people and standing up *for* people—whether it was defending a family member or cheering for the underdogs at the baseball field—was one part of their family culture.

So was a love of camping; being loud, opinionated, and sarcastic; pilgrimages to Tijuana to have an old VW, bought from newspaper classifieds, painted and reupholstered to resell; the importance of a side hustle (paper routes, babysitting, collecting aluminum cans, stenciling house numbers on curbs, etc.); being early adopters of new tech; and embracing and participating in big cultural moments (like the LA Olympics and Hands Across America).

Ben's family culture was deeply informed by his father's career: learning and teaching foreign languages. Partly because of this, Ben's childhood home often included weeks- and monthslong guests from other countries: Ecuador, Peru, Mexico, Mainland China, Taiwan, Mongolia, France, Finland, Russia, Lithuania, and more. His childhood was colored by these close encounters with people who came from very different cultures and often didn't speak much English. Ben and his siblings were encouraged to learn a few phrases like *hello*, *goodbye*, *what time is it?*, and *what is that?*, and how to count to ten in different languages. Ben learned that struggling to communicate didn't necessarily mean you couldn't or shouldn't try to understand or be understood.

Ben also remembers that his childhood home was more open to welcoming and hosting guests than most of his friends' homes, whether the guests were from other countries or not. Other things that were a part of Ben's family culture: singing together with piano accompaniment; collecting books (Ben's family was frugal with money, but it was always okay to splurge on a book); and showing what you knew or had learned (*Twenty Questions* and *College Bowl* were favorite family games). Video games were deemed a waste of time—though this didn't stop Ben from spending a good chunk of change on *Super Mario Bros.* at the arcade. And a common saying reinforced by Ben's mom was "Blairs don't hate anyone." This extended to referees and opponents in sports. Ben's family wouldn't participate in booing at sporting events and even would applaud opponents' good plays.

Whether you're aware of it or not, you're actively creating a family culture for your own kids every single day. We all are. So take some time to consider what your family culture is, what you would like it to be, and how, with intention, you can direct and cultivate it.

It's a wonderful exercise to sit down and think about what you want your family culture to be. In five or ten years, if you asked someone to describe your family culture—a friend or a sibling or someone who has interacted a lot with your family—what would you want them to say? What would you want them to have noticed about your family?

When we think about the family culture we've tried to create, this is what we picture: a culture of enjoying and sincerely liking one another. A culture of inclusiveness—if we see someone feeling left out in any social situation, we try to make them feel welcome and included. An embrace of hard work—that no work is demeaning, and we shouldn't fear or avoid hard work. A culture of participation—we make the most of any activity we're doing. Appreciating where we live—seeking out the favorite local foods and landmarks, getting involved in the community. A culture of creativity and problem solving. A culture of interacting with all ages—being at ease talking with a toddler or a septuagenarian.

The work we put into thinking about and developing our family culture isn't something we do alone as parents. Our children are a big part of it as well. Each of our kids has pushed our family to new activities, and each has demonstrated an interest in building a supportive and encouraging family culture.

From 2012 to 2014, our family made a video series called *Olive Us*. We shot more than forty professional videos over three years. There were many reasons we were interested in making these videos: They were an opportunity for everyone to participate in a meaningful and rewarding activity, and we could have something permanent to show for it. They were an opportunity for our children to learn about the process of filmmaking, and what goes into a film, and we could promote messages and ideals that we hoped would reach our children and other viewers.

At the time we started the series, we had noticed that so many shows aimed at children and young teens (think of what's on the Disney Channel and Nickelodeon) portrayed siblings who were mean to one another—the default stance was that the siblings were always on one another's nerves, and there was usually some competitive, sarcastic undertone in all interactions. Though there was sometimes a momentary resolution to a skirmish between siblings at the end of an epi-sode, the overriding message was that *siblings are annoying*.

When we started making *Olive Us*, we wanted to normal-ize healthy and encouraging interactions between siblings. In one episode, one of the sisters makes a lemonade stand, and her brother comes to see how it is going. The sister is frustrated because she hasn't had a customer yet. If this were a typical show, the brother would likely make fun of her, point out the mistakes she made, and probably make his own lemonade stand to compete. Their competition would esca-late throughout the episode, with each sibling getting increas-ingly combative and annoyed with the other, until the very end, when they finally come to some resolution and conclude that they should still tolerate one another after all.

This is not how the *Olive Us* "Lemonade Stand" episode unfolds. Instead, the brother asks the sister how her lemon-ade stand is going, she expresses disappointment, and he suggests they take a break and see if they can come up with some ideas together to improve the situation. They talk with each other and their other siblings, and then work together to make a successful lemonade stand. And that's it.

The thing is, it doesn't feel strange or inauthentic for siblings to be supportive and encouraging. *Olive Us* was an effort to capture what we wanted to build in terms of a family culture. Many episodes portray siblings collaborating or shar-ing an experience and appreciating one another's company. And we don't portray this as strange or exceptional. We show these interactions as normal because they are, or should be.

Other aspects of the family culture we wanted to build were also showcased in the series—things like problem solving, appreciating where we live, the value of participation, a willingness to do hard work, and a culture of kindness and caring for one another.

Family culture is not a fixed, inflexible set of activities and behaviors. Kids grow up, their interests change, and circumstances do too. Establishing a family culture is not about controlling what matters to your family! But as parents, especially when your kids are young, you have a lot of influence on which experiences or values your family really leans into and embraces.

Also, consider that, for young kids, what they remember as beloved family traditions may be something that only happened a few times. Let's say you introduce a "family movie night," with some out-of-the-ordinary details—like a fancy popcorn bowl reserved only for family movie night and a special system for picking the movie (maybe the youngest gets to pick a submission out of a jar filled with favorite movies). And let's say you have this special family movie night three different times over the year. There's a good chance, thanks to time and memory and the funny way it works for young kids, it could feel like family movie night was a *big* part of their childhood.

Ben has often told our kids that his family *always* skied on Christmas morning and then opened presents in the afternoon. But as he looks back, the reality is the Christmas morning skiing probably happened twice, or maybe three times? But to Ben, it feels like this was a pillar of Christmas. And it's funny to think that his older siblings—all of whom had grown up and moved out before the skiing years—won't remember Christmas skiing as part of the family culture at all.

It doesn't need to take a lot to change your family culture either. Try a new activity as a family—take a hike on a new path, try oil painting, winter swimming, bird-watching, or take a music lesson. If one of these activities is a hit—meaning the whole family really enjoyed it—then do it again. And again. Maybe give some equipment related to the activity (like binoculars) for a birthday. Lean into it. After not too long, bird-watching (or whatever activity you've embraced) will be part of your family culture.

It's okay to introduce new activities or ideas, even if you can't predict if they'll be a hit. For our first Christmas as newlyweds, a couple of years before we had kids, Gabrielle made a holiday journal. The idea was that we would take turns writing an entry at the end of each holiday season with favorite memories, how the Christmas tree looked, if we traveled or hosted guests, stuff like that. And then it would get packed away with other holiday items and would be fun to read through when we brought it out again the following December. Gabrielle was picturing twenty years in the future and how fun it would be reading back over all those holiday memories.

The journal had a slow start. There were years when we had lots of very young children where we don't even remember bringing out the journal, and if we did write an entry, it was very short, and we were probably irritated that we felt pressure to write a paragraph or two. But then something happened. Our kids learned to read and write. They discovered the journal among the holiday books, and they *loved* it. They got a kick out of reading a note about the gifts they received as a baby, or how we spent a Christmas traveling to

Grandma's house. The kids took over the holiday journaling responsibilities and, some years, there are pages and pages of notes with lots of different writers contributing. Gabrielle hasn't felt pressure to add to the journal in decades.

It's great that the journal has become a family treasure, but if it hadn't, that would have been okay too. If we had attempted it and the family wasn't into it, then it would have been fine to let it go. We can't always tell which traditions will become important or meaningful, so it's okay to try things and find out.

While the holiday journal has had a twenty-nine-year life and counting, other meaningful family culture activities we've established weren't so long-lived. Starting around 2006, we began conducting interviews with the kids. The plan was that it would be quarterly, and that it would be one child with both parents. We would talk about how they were doing in different areas of their life (physically, socially, intellectually, and spiritually). It would be a chance for a child to report on how they were feeling, ask questions, bring up any concerns, or frustrations, or areas where they needed our help. We would respond to them or take notes with action items to address later. For many years this plan worked well. But there were other years we only managed to do interviews once. Eventually the interviews tapered off—we've only done them once in the last four years.

The needs of your family will change over time. When there were six kids at home, the interviews helped us keep track of things we might have missed in all the chaos of raising a large family with young children. These days, it's easier to keep track of what our kids at home need, and the interviews don't feel as important. If an activity that was informing your family culture has fulfilled its purpose, it's okay to retire it.

It's safe to assume everyone wants a positive family culture. But we may not know how to articulate what that looks like, or it may not be clear how to get there from wherever we are. If building or improving your family culture is important to you, start by talking with your kids about it. How would they describe your current family culture? How would they describe the family culture of another family they appreciate or admire? How do your kids wish your family culture was different? Happily, the pathway to that desired family culture is straightforward. Talk about it, write down what family members want the culture to be like, and come up with activities, traditions, movies, books, and projects that will reinforce the hoped-for family culture. And then revisit the conversation as often as you like, so that you can make adjustments.

HOW WORKING TOGETHER MAKES YOU CLOSER

In his early twenties, Gabrielle's brother, Jared, started a triathlon in their hometown. Creating a race is a huge undertaking—figuring out and measuring the route, getting city permissions, creating the branding and marketing, getting people signed up, arranging for volunteers and safety resources along the route, and on and on. Much of this work Jared handled throughout the year, behind the scenes. But when it was time for the actual race, as many of Gabrielle's siblings (and their spouses) as possible would gather in Gabrielle's hometown to help put on the event.

The siblings would jump in to do whatever was needed. Run errands and gather supplies? Sure thing. Up superearly to mark the route? You got it. Make a playlist for the starting line? On it. Manage the T-shirt booth? You bet. Staff the water stations? Count on it. There wasn't a task the siblings were unwilling to tackle. And these were years when most of the siblings had very young children, so everyone was doing the triathlon tasks while also handling childcare and making sure the littlest ones were fed and occupied.

Ben loved getting to help at the triathlon and spending time with Gabrielle's brothers (who had become his good friends), and our own kids loved getting cousin time. Gabrielle felt so proud of her siblings and the way they could draw the community together and create a memorable event out of nothing. When the Stanley siblings were working together, they were their best selves—supportive, encouraging, enthusiastic, inclusive, and welcoming. They were like a magnet for others—people wanted to hang out and be around this positive and creative family.

Working together as a family is a core childhood memory for Gabrielle, and something she has prioritized with our own kids. Even as an adult, Gabrielle's favorite times spent with her siblings all involve working together on something meaningful, and happily, because the siblings are serial entrepreneurs, there have been many, many opportunities for the siblings to work together on new projects.

Since our return to France, the family projects with our own kids have centered on renovation tasks. Things like peeling wallpaper, removing old plaster, taking out rotted wood floors, and restoring stone walls. Many of these tasks have been recorded and shared on Instagram, and the comments are always a mix of excitement about the renovation project and wonderment at how we get our kids—actual teenagers—to participate. So many people asked: What was the secret?

We couldn't think of a secret, but we studied how we approached these projects, and realized we definitely had a system in place. Here's what has worked for us:

Manage their expectations. Before starting a project that will demand a lot of time or effort, let them know what the plan is in advance. Don't wake them up early on Saturday with no warning: *Get up! Time to clean out the garage!* Talk to them about it before it happens. Little kids need less warning. *After this show, in about fifteen minutes, we're going to clean up the toy room.* Older kids need more warning: *Have you noticed the garage is getting out of hand? What do you think of working together to tackle it on Saturday?*

Put a time limit on the task so they know how big of a project it is. This allows them to both manage their energy, and to plan around the project if they have other commitments that day. *We'll work from 10:00 a.m. to 12 p.m., and your time is free after that.*

Related to timing: If you have teens, they need sleep, so plan a later start. Family projects are not meant to torture or punish, they are meant to be a fun activity.

Tell your kids what the project will entail. *We're going to move every item out of the garage, sweep and dust, build these storage racks, and then put everything back in an organized way. Anything we don't have space for or don't really use anymore, we'll take to the donation center/junkyard.* Or: *We're going to clear the table, put the leftovers away, fill the dishwasher, scrub the pots and pans, wipe down the table and countertops, and sweep the floor.*

Prep in advance. Have everything you need for the project before your start time. If you're going to be digging up the yard, have enough tools and rakes and trowels and gloves on hand so that everyone can participate. If people gather, ready to work, and you have to delay to get supplies, it can suck the energy out of the project.

Work *with* your kids. Don't give an assignment and walk away, then come back and pass judgment on the project. Work *with* them. This is a *family* activity. Plan on working twice as hard as any of your kids. You know what you're doing, and you're an adult; your kids don't know what they are doing, and they are just kids. Also, this is *your* project; it's something important to *you*. Your kids may end up benefiting from this project and taking some pride in the work, but it's not theirs, they are not in charge of it. It's *your* thing. You need to care the most and work the most.

When the work begins, make sure everyone has a doable task, something at their skill level. Model how to do it. Model it over and over again if needed. If you're not sure how to do it, try to figure it out together. Try their ideas, have them look up a YouTube video, etc.; problem-solve together.

Make it fun. Have music playing. You could ask one of the kids to DJ as part of the project (keeping a happy vibe going is an important job). Come up with mental games or word games you can play while you work. Our kids like to imagine a ride at Disneyland and then think of how it would change if you themed it with a different movie. Kind of random, but it occupies their imagination and makes the work go quickly.

Take breaks when you are tired. Celebrate when a tricky part of the task is accomplished. Don't be grumpy—let your kids see you *enjoying* the project, and how happy you are to get it done. Don't criticize your volunteer helpers—shower them with compliments and show them how much you appreciate their contributions.

End when you said you'd end. If there's a bit more work, you can acknowledge it's ending time and ask if anyone is up for helping to finish. But if they're not up for it, respect that and finish the job yourself, or reschedule for another time.

Admire your family's work. This is very important. Ask everyone involved to stand back and admire the work. Note specific things about it that are improved. Give compliments about what each person accomplished. Don't skimp on this. Take some photos, bring them up again later in the day and admire the work again.

One of our favorite tools for admiring our family's work is the time-lapse feature available on most phones today. This feature allows you to set up your phone to record video for a long period of time (we think periods of fifteen to thirty minutes are optimal) and then it saves the footage as a short video where the work is sped up. Watching thirty minutes of work happen in under a minute feels like magic.

Mary Poppins provided a great example of the benefits of time-lapse in the scene when Mary helped Jane and Michael Banks tidy up the nursery using magic. This changed the task from drudgery to "a spoonful of sugar." Try it with any task that has a big visual impact—cleaning up a room, organizing the LEGOS or a bookshelf, peeling wallpaper or putting up wallpaper, doing the dishes, or making cookies. When your child watches the time-lapse video, it's much easier to see and understand what was accomplished during the project. Knowing there is a time-lapse video being created, they'll be more willing to work on future tedious projects.

Celebrate! You did something hard. Now celebrate. Maybe it's a scoop of ice cream. Maybe it's a family walk around the town pond. Maybe it's a board game. Celebrate together and thank your kids for their hard work. It doesn't have to be a big celebration; it doesn't have to cost any money. It could be any activity your child looks forward to. But whatever it is, make it clear the celebration is because of the family project. *We worked hard! Let's celebrate our hard work—how about we read aloud a chapter of* A Series of Unfortunate Events?

If you start this process with projects like cleaning up the toys or doing the dishes, your kids will learn to trust that family projects are really enjoyable experiences—even when they are challenging. They know that if they participate in a family project it will be fun, there will be laughing and singing and playing games while you work. They know they will be praised and appreciated. They know it will feel great to see and admire what they accomplished. They know you, the parent, will be right there, working with them and spending time with them. They know the family will celebrate afterward.

If your kids trust that when you suggest a family project, it will be a positive experience, we've learned there will be little resistance about participating (though not zero resistance; see the next chapter). As your kids grow, they will also instigate projects where they enlist the family's help—like a science fair project or an Eagle Scout project—and you can approach these projects in the same way, but now let your child lead, while you are an enthusiastic volunteer helper.

Whether you're working on big projects (like a renovation) or small projects (like basic chores), working together is one of the very best ways we've found to bond and build a strong relationship with our kids.

WHY WE DON'T EXPECT OUR CHILDREN'S BASELINE EMOTION TO BE HAPPY

Despite our efforts to manage collaborative projects with our kids (described in the previous chapter), they aren't always enthusiastic. And that's okay. As part of remodeling our current home, we have spent many Saturday mornings filling and then hauling rubble bags to the déchetterie—the very organized town dump, with specific drop-off points for metal, yard waste, recyclables, and so on. In the throes of consecutive rubble bag–filling weekends, one of our kids exclaimed that they weren't in the mood to fill rubble bags.

There are many reasons why someone would be excused from helping fill rubble bags (or another family activity): sickness, a conflicting event to attend or prepare for, etc. We work to manage expectations on activities that demand a lot from everyone. But "not being in the mood for it" is not really a valid excuse in our family. (Who is ever in the mood to fill rubble bags?!) Our response to someone who is not in the mood is something like: *That's okay. You don't have to be in the mood in order to help out.* And that is how we responded to this child. We didn't expect them to magically change their mood or outlook—but we still expected them to participate.

We don't put a lot of stock in ensuring that our children feel happy, or exhibit "positive" emotions at a given moment, or as a default emotional setting. Are you always happy? Of course not. We're not either. One thing we've noticed with our six kids is that each has a different emotional baseline. One is usually excited and upbeat while another is usually calm and serene. We've learned that our kids bring different moods and emotions at different times to the table, and we try not to expect or insist on the same baseline from everyone.

Our feelings are just that: feelings. It can be tempting to categorize feelings as "positive/good" (like happiness, joy, pride) and "negative/bad" (like sadness, anger, frustration), and conclude that we should seek to maximize the "positive" feelings and minimize the "negative" ones. But feelings aren't really like that. Feelings aren't *bad* and therefore to be avoided, or *good* and therefore to be sought after; feelings just *are.* Feelings are more like facts. A loved one dies, and we feel sadness and grief and maybe anger. We get rejected from a program we worked hard to apply to, and we feel disappointed, frustrated, or defeated. Not every emotion can or should be immediately metabolized into something more palatable.

We can feel "happy" in response to simple events like seeing a beautiful sunset, hearing birds sing, smelling a fragrant flower, or learning it will be a cloudless night when we have scheduled to watch the Perseids meteor shower. We can respond in a way that lets us appreciate these moments, like putting down our work to watch the sunset and remembering to literally smell the roses. But happiness is a fleeting feeling—all feelings are—and largely out of our control. We can't engineer these feelings of happiness to happen as frequently as we might like, and we certainly can't do it for our children.

While we don't see our work as parents to be constantly monitoring our child's feelings, and working to ensure they are positive, at least a part of our work *is* to help our child to participate in meaningful work. For us, projects we work on together as a family are good models for the role of emotions: We're not always happy when we work together on a project. And "being happy" is not an aim of our collaborative work. After all, the work usually involves difficult, objectionable, or tedious tasks (like clearing out an attic, removing wallpaper, cleaning out a drain, or taking a load of heavy bags to the dump). In the course of doing this work, we routinely run into frustrating complications and setbacks, and frequently enough we discover another involved project we'll need to tackle that we hadn't planned on, like when we were preparing to sand the floor in a room, only to discover that the floor needed to be replaced entirely. Our expectations aren't related to a child's emotions, but rather to their participation. We try to show them how to participate and expect them to contribute meaningfully.

The result of working together is usually increased competence in the specific work involved and competence working with one another. At the end of the best projects, when we can all see the difference our work has made, we experience a sense of satisfaction and fulfillment together. While this satisfaction is rewarding and can be a partial motivator for future projects, it is definitely not the predominant feeling throughout. It is not the reason or justification for the work. It is mostly reserved for the very end. And there are plenty of projects with no collective cheer of satisfaction at the end. But that's okay. It's a bad bargain to exchange the expectation of a continued feeling that is by nature fleeting, for an enduring relationship.

If we are overly concerned that our kids feel happy all the time, we might not ask them to participate in the difficult work where the sense of satisfaction and fulfillment comes only at the end. A more serious risk to insisting that a child is *always* happy, or believing that, ideally, a child should always or usually be happy—beyond its futility—is that it can ironically convey the message to our child that their "happiness" is a condition of our relationship. A much more valuable message to communicate with our children is that, because of our many shared experiences across a range of activities and emotions, we can trust and be at ease with one another, independent of our feelings.

One message that depression (which we have personal experience with) communicates that is true is that life is hard. We all experience distress at work or school. We'll run into relationship drama. Our feelings will be hurt. We'll have to deal with pangs of regret because of things we said or did. We'll feel lonely, self-conscious, and bored. Along with these everyday hardships, there is also a lot of real horror in the world. While violence and suffering have thankfully decreased over time, today, we're much more aware of incidents of violence and suffering than we ever could have been before. Across the political spectrum, people, including children, have become increasingly worried or pessimistic about the future of politics, and political rhetoric has stoked these fears (even if only when imagining the opposing party winning).

We don't mean to be dramatic about this or to suggest that we should expect all children to be Eeyores, but this context can be a helpful check if we'd assumed that our children should always, or usually, be happy. There will be times when your child feels crummy about their future and that's valid. They get to feel that, and we don't have to try to take those bad feelings away, even if it can be trying to sit with someone who is experiencing "negative" feelings.

There may be, and we should work toward bringing about, a future day when it is difficult to feel anything but deep satisfaction with the present, and eternal optimism about the future for everyone, but that day has not yet arrived. We sometimes feel despair, and it's a safe bet that your child will too.*

---

* An important clarification: There is a difference between "not feeling happy" at a given moment or on a given day on the one hand, and constantly feeling like life is not worth living on the other—whether the lasting depression is related to one's mental health or triggered by traumatic events or both. Not feeling happy at a given moment is normal; constantly wanting to not be alive is depression and needs medical intervention. If you or your child is depressed, you should seek professional help.

HOW TO USE YOUR HOME TO CREATE THE LIFE YOU WANT

When Ben was in graduate school, studying philosophy and education, he came across a passage from renowned educator and philosopher John Dewey on the role of the environment.

> *We never educate directly, but indirectly by means of the environment. Whether we permit chance environments to do the work, or whether we design environments for the purpose makes a great difference. . . . An intelligent home differs from an unintelligent one chiefly in that the habits of life and intercourse which prevail are chosen, or at least colored, by the thought of their bearing upon the development of children.*

This quote stuck with him and ended up having a big impact on our family. Because Gabrielle had studied design, and even wrote a book about home design, how our house looked and how it was put together naturally fell within her wheelhouse. But this Dewey quote got Ben thinking about home design through the lens of parenting and what it meant to create a good home environment. And from that point on, before Gabrielle made decisions about couch placement or where the bookshelves should go, we would discuss another kind of design goal: What activities did we want to happen in each space? How could we design the space to encourage the activities we wanted to happen in that room?

Creating environments in our home that reflect our values and the activities we want our family to engage in has become a lifelong project. And the power and possibilities in shaping an environment changed the way we look at the built world around us. For example, we think back to one day we were sitting on the bleachers while our kids were in a gymnastics lesson—a daughter doing impressive cartwheels on a balance beam, a son doing an involved routine on the rings, and we both experienced such a strong urge to get out there and use all that equipment—rings, bars, balance beams, a pommel horse, vaults, a bouncy, springy floor, and pits full of foam pieces where you can land when you practice your flips and dismounts. Outside of this gym, we are not usually fighting the urge to cartwheel. But the whole gym environment was inviting us—practically begging us—to run, jump, cartwheel, somersault, swing, and flip.

Sitting in the gymnasium we were reminded with force: *With the right environmental shaping, we can promote nearly any activity*. Ballerinas do barre work in a ballet studio; it's convenient to make a ceramic bowl in a pottery atelier; it's easy to work on an engine in an auto shop. But it's not easy, or advisable, to do any of those activities in other environments.

And once we understand and acknowledge how influential an environment can be, we can apply the same idea to our homes.

So parents designing a home can start by asking questions like: *In our home, which activities and conversations are already taking place? Which ones seem to take place naturally? Which ones do we wish would take place but currently don't? How big is the gap between the activities that actually take place and those we wish would take place?* And then we can make changes to our home based on those answers.

If we wanted to see more reading, we should consider our bookshelf situation and note whether our book selection is enticing and if our comfiest seating has a good lamp within reach. If we want to see more building or engineering happening, we can ask: *Is there a convenient and highly visible worktable with tools at hand?* If we want our young kids to feel independent in the kitchen, and be able to fix themselves a snack, then imagining what snacks they would want to prepare, and storing what they need on lower shelves that they can easily access will get us closer to that goal.

We're no Von Trapp family singers, but we really enjoy singing songs as a family, while one or more of us accompanies the vocals on guitar. Keep in mind we haven't paid more than two hundred dollars for any guitar (most were under thirty dollars), and none of our children is a guitar virtuoso. That's never been the priority. Everything we hoped to get out of our guitar purchases and guitar practicing is realized in these jam sessions.

But these jam sessions weren't inevitable. We used to keep our most expensive guitar in a hard-back case—this offered protection, but it also added an extra step to any proposed jam session (the extra step = getting the guitar out of the case). For sheet music, we depended on printouts with guitar chords and lyrics, but using and storing the sheets got unwieldy, and it's safe to assume the printer would be out of ink or otherwise out of order at the moment of need. Printing our music and getting ready for a jam session always felt like a bit of a production—something we had to plan for and think about ahead of time. Because of this, jam sessions didn't happen very often—and could be as frustrating as they were fun.

But we really wanted these jam sessions to be a part of our family life, so over the years, we progressively made it easier and easier to make them happen. We started by making the guitars easier to access and put away—the room where we currently have jam sessions has several guitars of various sizes that any child can easily reach and play in a matter of seconds. They can be put away just as easily.

For this to happen, we had to decide that our guitars would not be precious. The guitars don't need protection or special treatment. The kids do not need to be supervised while using them. We do not have special guitar hooks—we attach simple ribbons and hang the ribbons on a picture hook. The kids can move them around the house when needed—maybe bring them to their room so they can practice while lounging on the bed. We can send the guitars with the kids to camp or college dorm rooms (we keep their cases in the attic in case the guitars need to travel). If they get scratched, it's not a big deal. If they break beyond repair, we can have fun hunting for a replacement at garage sales. This accessibility made a huge difference for our family. It increased the amount of guitar practice that happened in our house, and it increased the frequency of our jam sessions.

For sheet music, the improvements and accessibility happened because of new tech. The guitar chord iPhone apps were game changers. At first, we would keep our set list to songs we all knew the words to, and the guitarist would read the music off a phone held up by a singer. Or for a new song, we could all look at separate phones, or hover around the guitarist. This was a huge improvement over the paper sheet music, but we eventually figured out how to make it even better. These days, we screencast the guitar music app from our phone to the TV—the app includes the chords and the lyrics. So now, everyone in the room can easily see the chords and sing or play along. We need only one phone, and even for new songs, everyone can join in the singing.

With instantly available music and lyrics that everyone can see, featuring every song we could ever think of, plus guitars within an arm's reach, our jam sessions happen naturally and frequently. These sessions take no planning or preparation; they can, and do, happen at a moment's notice. They can involve as many or as few family members as are interested and available at that moment.

Some activities become much easier just by adding a prop. An example of this is our household podium. We've had one since before we had kids. Ben happened to own one when we married, and we used it to host lecture nights where our friends would gather and one of them would deliver a talk about one of their interests—the Beatles and the pituitary gland are two examples of lecture topics from that era of our lives. We eventually said goodbye to that podium during a cross-country move but replaced it with a new one that was size-appropriate for kids. It has received so much use! It's where our kids have practiced for school presentations or church talks, we've used it for family meetings, we've used it for parties, we've used it for plays.

Having a podium has made it easier for our kids to get comfortable with public speaking—it's probably some kind of psychological trick, but standing at a podium is like having permission to hold forth like a professional orator, instead of defaulting to shyly mumbling with your head bowed. Or maybe it's just easier to picture yourself giving a speech when you're standing at a podium.

So a simple physical prop can help certain activities happen, but what about something more abstract? What if you want an environment where your children share frustrations and successes about school or their social life? How can we get our home to be more conducive to this? We might set up the space so it feels natural to converse. Think comfortable seating—side-by-side options and facing options, a shared table, a dish for holding simple snacks, a basket of cozy blankets. We could deliberately reward sharing—we could post images or language on the wall to help with this, like a picture of a child talking to attentive parents, or a sheet of paper that lists phrases like "Thank you for sharing!" "I love learning about your frustrations and successes." "I really appreciate that you shared that with me," etc. We could keep a journal noting past frustrations and successes with school or our social life, or we could make an easily replayable recording of our discussions that we can keep cued up to share.

We could have a mantra displayed that reads something like: WE VALUE SHARING FRUSTRATIONS AND SUCCESSES IN SCHOOL AND SOCIAL LIFE IN THEIR OWN RIGHT. We could put up a sign that reads: ESPECIALLY IN THIS ROOM, I'M INTERESTED IN HEARING ABOUT YOUR FRUSTRATIONS AND SUCCESSES WITH SCHOOL OR SOCIAL LIFE. Or we could do something a little less direct.

Here are some sample design decisions we made to encourage specific activities or behaviors:

We made the kids' bedrooms relatively boring. Toys and tech and TVs were all kept in shared spaces like the living room. Most of our books were also on shelves in shared spaces. We designated bedrooms for sleeping and changing clothes (yes, of course, there were a few books on the nightstand—we're not monsters). The idea was that this would encourage the kids to spend more time out of their rooms, interacting with siblings and hanging out together as a family. And it worked! (No judgment if you prefer the opposite and your family loves the max amount of alone time—we're all allowed to value different things.)

We fixed or replaced irritating items we had to interact with frequently. Like the trash can with the pedal where the lid didn't close properly, or the table that was just slightly too big and stuck out too far and made it easy to stub your toe. Frustrations can compound over the course of lots of interactions with items like that, and frustrations can turn into bad moods or trigger lashing out at fellow family members.

We tried to make creativity easily accessible. For two and a half years, we rented the home of an artist—which included an artist's studio. We rented the home fully furnished and the studio came with a huge stack of large poster-size white card stock—maybe two feet by three feet—and we had permission to use as much as we wanted. We'd always had art supplies around, but it was so interesting to see how much having a big supply of big paper and a big space in which to use it made the projects the kids came up with grow. It's like the huge stack of paper let their brains think bigger. We remember one of our kids, age six at the time, cut out a series of oversize horses as big as he was. We haven't always had a studio space our kids could use, but it was a good reminder about how our environment affects our actions.

A quick note here to point out: None of this requires a big home, or a home with many rooms. Occasionally, a new piece of furniture or another item can help. But the home design we're talking about isn't expensive. It is obviously not tied to designer labels, or fancy props. It may just be about removing distractions. Mostly it's about gaining clarity on which activities and conversations you want to encourage, and then adapting your home environment accordingly.

Think of it this way: As a parent, you have in effect hired your home to help you promote certain activities and conversations and discourage others. In fact, your home is already helping you to facilitate and promote whatever you and your family actually do at home—whether you planned it or not. If you are not doing the activities and having the conversations you wish you were, part of the solution is to take this up with your home. If your home is not working with you or helping you as you'd like, the solution is not to lament this, complain about uncooperative kids, insist on obedience, or feel like you've failed as a parent, but may be to just tend to your home environment.

HOW TO
MANAGE
SCREEN
TIME

Most parents we talk to have

a general fear or dread of "too much screen time" hanging over their family. We've felt the same fear and dread and have probably spent too much time thinking about screen time.

We had a dozen years of parenting and six kids before our house experienced its first iPad in 2010 (or was it 2011?). Because of that, it's hard for us to see screens as a "bad" thing. To us, the iPad felt like a miracle.

At that time, there was practically a whole industry on how to travel with kids, and it wasn't about where to stay or what activities to do—it was about how to keep kids entertained during flights and long car rides. There were DIY projects and how-tos and much discussion among parenting bloggers of which kid-travel-hacks worked and which didn't. Gabrielle remembers spending hours prepping for family vacations, trying to come up with activity kits for each kid to keep them occupied during road trips. She absolutely dreaded the (rare) flights we took because managing the kids was so exhausting. We remember discussing whether it was harder to be the driver or harder to manage the kids' snacks and entertainment on a drive, and both wishing we could call dibs on driving.

And then, we, and many other parents, started experiencing travel with an iPad, and that whole how-to-travel-with-kids conversation *disappeared*. Screens made really challenging parts of parenting so much easier! We weren't asking questions about how much screen time is too much screen time, we were asking: How long until the baby can hold and manage a screen themselves? We would not wish the challenges of those pre-screen days on any parent, and we know that our experience colors our opinions on screens.

So does this bias mean we believe there should be no limits on screen time for kids? We think this type of rhetorical question masks the real issues. For young kids, American childhood is usually quite busy—there may be trips to the park, and visits to Grandma's house, and circle time at the community center, and neighborhood dogs to say hello to, and playdates, and preschool, and toy LEGOs to build, and nap time, and lunchtime, and snack time. If a child is squeezing screen time in there, too, that's probably not something to worry much about.

But maybe the bigger issue is: What exactly are we talking about when we say screen time? Are we bothered that our twelve-year-old is reading books on a Kindle instead of in paper format? Are we trying to cut down on the amount of reading they are doing? Are we concerned when our kids are building a world or an object in *Minecraft*—an act of problem solving and creating? Are we saying we want less of that? Are we stressed when our kids are watching hand-lettering tutorials for Procreate and drawing lettering designs on the iPad? Are we troubled when our kids like keeping a digital journal (like a blog) instead of a hand-written journal? Are we furrowing our brows because our kids are looking up facts online about Australia for a report? Are we worried about how often we're sitting down as a family to watch a movie? Does that count in our mental calculations of too much screen time?

When we discuss too much screen time with each other and with other parents, the answer is: no—the sorts of examples we've just listed are not what parents are concerned about. In fact, most people agree that screens have allowed for wonderful experiences for their families. A nonverbal child with autism may rely on their iPad for communication. That's amazing! A tween has learned to edit short videos and made birthday movies for each member of the family. What a treasure! A family has bonded over PowerPoint parties where they make and present funny or interesting slideshows for one another based on a theme. Delightful! Grandparents who live far away get to video chat with their grandkids and read them bedtime stories. It's miraculous! During dinnertime discussions about the school day or current events or history, families can look up maps or data or news stories instantly. Unbelievably cool! Screens have enabled both of us to work from home with flexible schedules, and that has made a huge difference for our family. To us, screens have been a major blessing!

So if our collective parenting concerns aren't truly about too much screen time, then what are they about? When we've drilled down in these conversations, there are some specific fears and concerns we've discovered (let's discuss some of those below), and then an overall sort of vague feeling of distrust directed toward new technologies and cultural changes. This feeling of distrust seems understandable to us, and likely every generation of parents has experienced something similar; we can't look into the future and see if the technological changes of our day are going to cause problems for our children's futures, so we treat these changes with suspicion.

Over the years, we've tried to tackle the specific screen-related fears, and work through the overall fear of too much screen time—partly because we needed to deal with a specific problem, and partly because we just weren't willing to be constantly stressed out about screen time.

For specific concerns, we tried to pinpoint the problem without just blaming screens or demanding no more screen time. At one point, it felt like screen time was interfering with a good night's sleep for one of our kids. So we came up with a plan to collect all the device chargers in the house and set up a charging station in our bedroom. The kids would check in their screens at bedtime for charging, and could pick them up in the morning, recharged and ready to go. The issue we were trying to overcome was someone not getting enough sleep. And we suspected eliminating screens at bedtime would solve it, or at least help. (But we also knew it could have been some other issue or stress that was keeping them up, and that removing screens could have meant they would stay up late doing something else. We tried to stay focused on solving the sleep problem and not assume it was a screen problem.)

Another specific fear was online abuse or bullying via social media. There are so many terrifying articles featuring instances of abuse and if you read the news at all, it's basically impossible to avoid them, so, of course, parents get worried about this, and we were not immune. We managed our concerns around this specific fear in three ways:

1) Based on what we read, the worst of the abuse seems to happen in middle school, so we came up with a plan to not allow smartphones until high school. Granted, that was easier to do when there were more phone options that weren't smartphones—kids could still text or call without having access to apps in their pocket.

2) We also followed the guidelines set by the apps—if thirteen was the minimum age, we didn't allow for an Instagram account until thirteen. And if thirteen came along and they weren't asking for Instagram, we didn't feel compelled to introduce it or bring it up at all; there's no need to make a big deal of it like, "Hey it's your thirteenth birthday, let's sign you up for Instagram!" If they did want to sign up, we let them have only a private account and allow only followers they knew in real life.

3) We talked to our kids directly about our fear: *Hey, social media can be a lot of fun, but sometimes there are creepy people who reach out. Maybe they will ask you to do something dangerous and threaten to hurt your parents or your siblings if you don't do it. They are lying, and they aren't safe people, so you need to tell us about that. And it's not just you, creepy people reach out to us too. It's not your fault and you don't need to be embarrassed about it. Just tell us.*

Another specific fear (related to the previous one) is not knowing what your kids are accessing online. There are parental control software options you can use, and you can limit their phone privacy and do safety check-ins (if they are sending or receiving inappropriate pics from peers, that's illegal!). But we think our best response to this fear is instituting family screen time. We think of it as the current version of gathering to watch must-see TV on Thursday nights like previous generations got to do with their families. How it works: We gather in the family room the same way we might to watch a movie, but instead of all watching one big screen, we're all watching our own small screens. No headphones allowed. And we're sharing as we go. Someone's on TikTok and someone's on Instagram and someone's on YouTube and someone's on Twitch and we're sharing the latest post they made, or something funny they found, and we're laughing and reading tweets aloud and saying, *Oh, did you see this meme? Did you hear this news about your favorite musician's next album?* Instead of looking at a screen being an isolated activity, it's something enjoyable we're doing together.

Another benefit of family screen time is that it's a chance to reinforce to your kids that everything they're seeing online, you're also seeing. If they're seeing memes and headlines about a news story, you're seeing them too—maybe a slightly different version is being shared on Instagram from what's on TikTok, but the messaging is basically the same. Sometimes kids think that their parents have no idea what's going on in the world that the kids or teens are living in. But family screen time can correct that notion. Plus, it helps you learn what your kids are interested in and what's making them laugh. It helps you understand what your kids are getting out of screen time and is a chance to watch for any red flags.

Rather than worrying about too much screen time, we focus on introducing screen time opportunities that are positive and creative.

When blogging was in its heyday back in the aughts, our kids who were old enough to read started free Blogspot blogs. We still have the URLs and look up the blog posts from time to time and they are a family treasure. The topic of one memorable post, "My Favorite Blues," featured a list of different blues, which included among eleven options, "glittering dark blue," "middle blue," "ocean blue," and "lightest blue in the world." These blogs were shared with cousins and friends and grandparents who could comment and interact. The blogs provided lots of positive feedback to budding writers.

When we lived far from family, we used our kids' love of *Minecraft* as a way to bond with cousins. On Sundays, they would organize long Cousin *Minecraft* Sessions where they would all build and play together on a shared server. Years later, those *Minecraft* sessions were replaced with Cousin *D&D* Sessions.

When the kids wanted a gaming system, we started with a Wii U and focused on games with lots of movement—like *Dance Dance Revolution*, and *Wii Sports*, or games that were fun to play with multiple players so four of us could play at once, and it could be a group activity. We followed game ratings and bought only age-appropriate and family-appropriate games.

During the Covid lockdown, we bought a refurbished iPad and Apple Pencil and designated it the drawing iPad. We removed as many apps as possible so that it was only used for Procreate, our favorite drawing app.

When *Wordle* came out, we all got into it and shared scores on the family text chat.

We host family PowerPoint parties a couple of times each year, where there's a theme and each person creates and presents a slideshow.

As mentioned earlier, we use screens for family jam sessions—we use an app on our phone to display the chords and lyrics on the TV, so we can all see them and play and sing together.

Basically, we've looked for ways to encourage creativity and learning on screens, so that when the kids are bored or craving screen time, we don't feel compelled to distract them with another activity, and instead can say, *What are you building in* Minecraft *right now? Go see how much progress you can make in an hour. What are you drawing lately? Can you design a sign for your sister's birthday? How far did you get in those keyboarding tutorials?*

We don't like the general assumption that screen time is horrible or a bad thing or bound to cause problems. We don't see how that's a helpful stance to take. Having access to all the world's knowledge in a little device is incredible. And beyond that, we both use screens all day, every day, for work. Every desk job does as well, and a lot of other jobs too. Because we work at home, our kids see us using our screens for work every day—we don't want them to fear screens but to understand them as a tool for work and creativity. We want the baseline to be: Screens aren't essential for lots of things, but they are a useful part of life.

If your own kids are getting themselves down over social media comparisons, one solution could be to get off the triggering platform. Another could be to dive deeper into making content so that your kids understand what goes into what they're seeing and that what they're seeing may be as fake as any scripted TV show. Take a weekend and plan out an awesome video, and what it should be about; gather props from around the house, decide on an outfit, do hair and makeup, record lots of takes until you feel like you've got a few you're happy with, edit the video on TikTok or Instagram, working with the allowed time limits. Add music. Then share it with friends and family.

If you do this, maybe they'll love it and have fun creating additional videos. But even if they don't love the process of making the video, or even if the video doesn't turn out quite how they expected, they'll learn a few things: They'll learn that everything they're seeing on social media is pretend. They'll know how much time these social media people are spending on hair and makeup and planning outfits. They'll know that despite the hair and makeup work, there is still a filter that changes their looks even more—that the faces they are seeing are not reality. They'll understand that this "casual" video they are seeing may represent many hours of work, and many takes, and lots of editing; that someone could have spent four days making a thirty-second TikTok.

Again, if they love making the video, they'll know this is an option, that it just takes lots of time and work and that with practice people get better at it. If they don't love it, they'll know not to be jealous of the creators they are watching—they'll know the videos they see require lots of work. They'll know that even if you put in lots of work, the video you make may get only a few likes, or no reaction at all; the amount of hours spent doesn't translate into views or money.

This seems like valuable knowledge for any child who is both interested in and stressed out by social media. Taking your kids through an exercise like that (*let's try to make the best video we can make with the time and the resources we have*) makes it really clear that the vast majority of what we're seeing online is an intentional creation, not a snapshot of unedited reality.

We realize the general dread around too much screen time that parents experience is just the most recent form of a problem that has been going on forever. When we see people feel an urgent need to eliminate screens from their kid's life, we understand the instinct, but we also think of it as the modern version of the parents who wouldn't allow their Gen X kids to watch TV. We understand there were some pros and cons for those kids. Pros: Maybe they wrote in their journals more, or spent more time outside, or had to come up with creative ways to spend their free time. Cons: They often felt socially ill at ease—they weren't seeing the *SNL* skits or sitcoms that were being talked about at school and couldn't relate. As adults they still have some cultural blind spots. And yes, anytime they went to a friend's house, they would want to do nothing but watch TV. Television became a forbidden treasure they could seek after. We know the parents felt like they were doing their kids a big favor by not allowing TV, but it's unclear whether those kids, now adults, appreciated the favor then or now.

After "TV is going to rot their brains," our culture experienced "video games are going to rot their brains," and now we're in the middle of "too much screen time is going to rot their brains." Along those lines we wonder: If a modern parent tried to eliminate screen time for their kids now, in the same way that a 1970s parent might have tried to eliminate TV watching, what would that even mean? No smartphone? No TV? No family movie night? No computer for doing homework? For schools, so much communication with students happens through online platforms, so a no-screen life may not even be possible. If a parent was able to accomplish such a thing, would there be pros and cons? Sure. But as far as we can see, it's not clear at all that the pros would outweigh the cons.

We also take into account that if too much screen time ends up creating a future outcome that is negative for our kids, it won't just affect our kids, it will affect approximately *eight billion people*. That means it won't be a personal problem to solve, it will be a cultural and a technological shift that the whole world will be dealing with.

If our kids were somehow in the 1 percent of humanity who is not dealing with the problem, we're not sure that would actually be a benefit for our kids.

In our experience, worrying about too much screen time—which we have definitely done—is misplaced worry and wasted energy. If there's a specific screen-related problem your kids are experiencing, you can deal with that specific problem. But worrying about a vague outcome of too much screen time that we don't know will even happen is unnecessary.

HOW TO
RESPOND
WHEN YOUR CHILD
REJECTS
YOUR
RELIGION

It used to be a safe bet that a child would continue to participate in their parent's religious community into adulthood. This is no longer a safe bet. A decade or so ago, when all our kids were still at home, we came across an article reporting on a trend of younger generations opting out of religious participation, across faiths. As religious people ourselves, and as parents of kids who span the entirety of Gen Z (our oldest is among the oldest of Gen Z kids, and our youngest is among the youngest), we were of course curious about these findings. It spurred an important conversation between the two of us. What would we do if one of our children decided not to practice our religion? It was a quick discussion, and we easily decided that we would not let our religion get in the way of our relationship with our children. We will always love our children far more than our religious beliefs.

Though we were both born and raised in the Mormon church, our families have landed in different places during our adulthood. Ben's siblings are all still actively practicing

Mormonism, though the majority have at least one adult child who is no longer practicing. Among Gabrielle's siblings, only Gabrielle is still a practicing Mormon. This generational departure from the religion we were all raised in is understandably hard on parents who are still practicing.

For those who consider their religion to be an essential part of their identity, when their children don't want to participate, it can feel like judgment and personal rejection. On the side of the children, they feel their own sting of rejection—the feeling that their parents are more willing to give their time, attention, resources, and loyalty to an organization rather than their own child. We've seen parents and grandparents cut off relationships with children and grandchildren who leave the religion, and cultivate relationships only with the ones who stayed. We've seen children cut off their family altogether because they feel all communication is fraught with judgment and disappointment, or they turn family gatherings into a platform for disparaging their family's religion. We won't delve into the possible reasons for the generational shift away from religious practice but just present it as a fact, and explore how parents can respond in ways that minimize the harm and trauma on a family. We know this is a painful topic for many parents, and also for many children. And we're familiar with accounts of cruel behavior going in both directions. Though the discussion here may feel one-sided, this is a parenting book, so we are focusing on the behavior of parents—what parents can do and what mindset they can bring to improve these situations.

Not everyone agrees with our conclusion that we won't let our religion get in the way of our relationship with our children. They might bring up the story of Abraham and Isaac from the Old Testament as an admirable example of a parent willing to sacrifice their child for their religious beliefs. As you may know, in the story, God asks Abraham to kill his son, Isaac, as a demonstration of Abraham's faith in God, and his willingness to go through with this sacrifice made Abraham the revered "father of faith." It's a foundational story for Judaism, Islam, and Christianity, and biblical scholars have wrestled with it for centuries. As the story goes, Abraham prepares to kill Isaac, binding him to an altar, and raising his knife, with the intention to murder Isaac on God's order, when an angel stops him and explains that this was only a test of Abraham's faith, and Abraham passed the test.

For religious scholars, it's a nuanced myth that challenges preconceptions about God, ethics, family, and promises. For religious practitioners, it can be read as a story of the ultimate sacrifices one should be willing to make for their religion. For us personally, as parents, it's not a complicated story at all. We read it and can dismiss this God—or *any* God who would make such a request—out of hand. And we think anyone who feels compelled to obey such a request or feels the need to at least deliberate about such a request from anyone—including a god—should be dismissed as a fanatic.

When we see parents doubling down on their religious participation at the cost of their relationship with their child, we think a fitting response to Abraham almost killing Isaac is to ask: What God are we worshipping that would demand we reject our child in favor of *this* God? And, as parents, how could we justify such a god as worthy of worship?

This story has always been taught to us as a hypothetical test of faith. But in recent years, we've started seeing it in practice. There are parents who are choosing their religion over their kids. True, they're not killing their kids, but they are cutting them off or kicking them out of the home. Or their children believe that's what their parents want to do.

We don't agree with those parents, and we think they are wrong. If you, like us, have prioritized your children over your religious beliefs without abandoning those beliefs, or if you are not sure how to navigate a relationship with your child since they have rejected your religion, here's what we're offering in this essay: 1) an analogy that may comfort you, 2) a reminder that religion is just one part of who you are, and 3) a way to build bridges with your kids who choose to reject your religion.

First, the analogy. We find it helpful to think of religion as a gift that a parent can give to their child—a gift their child can choose to accept or not. This act of giving honors the value the religion has played in the parent's life and the desire of the parent to share that value with their child. But as anyone who has given a gift knows, the act of giving does not require the act of receiving or appreciating the gift. Just because we consider a gift to be valuable does not mean that the recipient will value it the same, or at all. A religious parent can honor their child's decision to accept the gift or not, and their child's response doesn't change the intent of the gift, or the value of the gift for the giver.

If you've raised your child in a specific religion, then your child knows what the religion is and what it offers. And if they ever want or need what the religion has to offer, they know how to access and participate in the religion. But we can't force others to feel as we do about the gifts we give them.

We understand that for a religious parent, this gift analogy may not relieve anxiety—a parent could be making a calculation that compares an eternity of joy to an eternity of misery. In such a calculation, they may feel there is no room for compromise or negotiation and conclude that the only way forward is to use every interaction to pressure the child back to the religion. If a parent is making this sort of bet, they may have the support of their religious community, but it can come at the expense of a healthy, flourishing relationship with their child.

Which brings us to identity. If your child leaving your religion is a source of anxiety, it likely means that your religion is a key part of your identity. And if that's the case, it could hurt to realize that your child's identity doesn't include something that is a big part of *your* identity. But even if it may feel like the essential core of your identity, it's still not your only identity. You are a parent. You are someone's child. You may be a sibling, an uncle or aunt, a teacher, a barber, a lawyer, a chess player, a lover of cheesecake. As important as it is to you, your religious identity is only one part of you—as essential as it may be. If your religious identity is interfering with your relationship with your child, you can always choose to focus on and develop one of your many other identities.

A related idea that may be of comfort: Even if your child leaves your religion, it will still be a part of who they are, part of their personal history—it just may be a much smaller part of their identity than it is for you. We appreciate that this can be painful. But this is part of what it means for a child to become an adult—they develop their own independent identity, and it will be different from yours in many areas.

Now let's build some bridges. Let's explore values that are encouraged in, but aren't specific to, your religion. Things like service, working to help or relieve oppressed populations, working toward a more just future, etc. When we lived in Oakland, our congregation worked with a small community organization, Emeryville Citizens Assistance Program (ECAP), that served meals to local populations in need. We would help distribute food at the ECAP center and to homeless encampments. Participants who joined us were not all active members of our church. In fact, many were people who had departed from Mormonism, and who would not be willing to participate in other religious observances, but who were happy to participate in this work with ECAP.

Something we value about our religious practice is the opportunity it brings to do this type of service. These kinds of activities can connect generations who may otherwise be disappointed in one another's religious beliefs. People can participate in these types of activities, whether or not they are responding to the same religious impulse.

As the article forecasted, we have, in fact, experienced adult children deciding to leave the religion we raised them in. This was not unexpected. One day, we received a letter from one of our kids, who was worried that their changing relationship to the church would change their relationship with us. Here's how we responded:

Dear Kid-We-Love,

We agree that the current focus of the church feels ill-suited for many of the pressing issues in the world today, and we resonate with the concerns you have shared about what issues and investments the church should prioritize.

We think there are great possibilities for the church, as modeled through efforts like ECAP, where individual members recognized a real, present need, worked to do something about it, and leveraged the church's resources (volunteers and money) to address it in a more powerful way. This is the way we have tried to practice and encourage the church to move forward through our actions, conversations, and writing, but we agree it doesn't seem to be the predominant message and effort of the church currently. We still see a lot of promise in the church with a focus on addressing real-world issues like poverty, starvation, etc.

We agree with you that community aspects (e.g., befriending lots of people from lots of backgrounds and ages) are some of the greatest strengths of the church. The church is a community where we can have an audience and can be influenced for good and can make a bigger difference in the world than we can as individuals. It's not the only one—as you know, we each belong to several other communities where we are very active—but it has taken a lot of effort and time to get to a place to have an influence in these other communities. This is not to say that you need the church, just that you have a ready community that can support you, and that you can influence should you want to—but to be clear, we wouldn't want to suggest this at the cost of your health or quality of life.

We are completely fine if any or all of our children choose to not associate with the church. We mean this sincerely. When we were younger parents we read the stats on how many people in our kids' generation were leaving religion (not just Mormonism, all religions); we discussed it and agreed that our relationship with our children would be the priority over any type of religious belief or activity.

We hope you already know this, but we will respect our children's choices and beliefs and love you all, unconditionally.

We don't expect you to attend church with us if we are attending. If a family member is speaking, or there is someone you want to see, perhaps you will want to come, and we hope that you will always feel welcome there, but we don't ever expect you to pretend to believe or participate out of a desire just to please us.

If the church isn't working for you, or for any of our children, we don't want to stand in the way of you finding a better life or balance.

We realize we have written some defenses of aspects we value about the church—we're not trying to be defensive or stand up for the church and oppose your decision but want to give a better picture of where we're coming from. But the overall message is that we love our children more than the church and want you all to live fulfilling lives, and if that means any or all of you don't want to associate with the church, we are one hundred percent fine with that.

Mostly, we love you and we're really glad that you are talking about this stuff with us. Please never hesitate to do so. It does not offend us even a little bit. Please consider this a permanently open conversation.

Love, Dad & Mom

HOW TO HELP YOUR CHILD LEAVE HOME

So far, every child moving out

has come as a shock. The most dramatic move (and we wouldn't recommend it for the faint of heart) was our fourth child. The university he wanted to attend doesn't send program acceptance notices until a few weeks before classes start, and while he was waiting to hear, he was still considering taking a gap year. When he received notice of acceptance, he took a week to make a decision: He decided to skip the gap year and enroll directly in university, which left us with two weeks to plan an international move and get him settled before freshman orientation and classes began.

But really, no matter how much warning we've had, or how long we've had to prepare, the moment the child moves out always feels like an abrupt surprise—like it came out of nowhere. Each and every time we've felt ourselves starting to panic: *Oh no! Have we actually prepared this child for independent living?*

The first time, it triggered a parenting shame cycle as we recognized that no matter how much we had taught them, we hadn't taught them every possible thing they would need to know. How many meals do they truly know how to prepare? How will they handle it if they don't get along with their roommate? Have they ever made a grocery list and done the shopping? Do they know what a budget is? How confident are we that they know how to thoroughly clean a bathroom? Do they have any idea how irritating it is that the dorm laundromat only takes quarters, and that they'll therefore need to keep quarters on hand? What if they need to dress up for something—should we be packing them a shoe-shine kit? Would they know how to use it if we did? Do they understand that even though it's bothersome, sometimes you really do have to deal with paperwork and red tape? Speaking of paperwork, what about taxes?! We forgot to teach them to do taxes!

So, in an attempt to calm our panic and bridge the knowledge gap, we've tried something we call "adulting boot camp."

What we teach in this boot camp depends on the specific child's needs and where they are heading. For the child who was leaving on a mission and would be wearing a suit, collared shirt, and dress shoes every day, it was important to review how to care for a suit, iron a shirt, and polish dress shoes. For the kid heading off to college, we might focus on time management, dorm etiquette, and tips for using the writing center and navigating the cafeteria. For the child heading off to be an au pair, we might brush up on first aid training, and come up with a list of quick kid-friendly meals, and ways to keep kids occupied while waiting in line.

Basically, we assume there are many behind-the-scenes tasks we do as parents that the child may not be aware of, and we bring those tasks to their attention. This is the time to reveal the family's secret blend of herbs and spices, how to remove a stubborn stain, change a tire, or replace a button. We have conversations about how to budget, how to manage a bank account, and what it means to have a healthy lifestyle.

This boot camp channels our worry about our child's readiness to leave the home and tries to add some structure to make it fun if a bit formal. We discuss which tasks, principles, and activities to focus on—determined by what the child will be doing in this next phase of their life—and approximately how much time to spend on each. Then we coordinate with our child to make a schedule where we spend time on each activity spread out over a weekend or a couple of weekends. We ask our child to really give some thought to how their life is going to be different, what it's going to look like, and what questions or worries they have about it. This also informs what we teach at boot camp.

A day of boot camp might look like a budgeting game in the morning using Monopoly money, then pulling out the iron to practice ironing shirts and pants, then going out for lunch, then reading and discussing an article about "things I wish I had known freshman year," then making a meal plan for a week, then learning to cook a favorite recipe for dinner.

The structure of the boot camp lends itself to inviting outside help. For example, if you're doing a boot camp for a child who will need to maintain a car, and your sister is really good at car maintenance and you aren't, you could include two hours of car maintenance skills with Aunt Rachel as part of boot camp.

Boot camp can be an involved thing with a thought-out, prearranged, printed schedule, perhaps coordinated with other adults who are helping out. But it doesn't have to be elaborate at all. It can be as simple as communicating to your child: *Here are some facts and skills I don't feel like I've taught you yet.* And then modeling or discussing each skill. At our house, how we've approached this with each kid has often come down to what our schedules look like at the time. Sometimes it's very low-key because that's all we have bandwidth for. Other times it will feel more structured, and the younger siblings will want to be involved as well, with everyone playing a budgeting game together. If there's an activity the child seems annoyed by, we can skip it and remind ourselves that none of this is meant to be stressful.

Other benefits of adulting boot camp, besides teaching them some actual principles and skills in a lighthearted, low-stakes environment, include that it's a clear indication and communication to our child that they are about to cross an important threshold, but they're not done learning and growing. It's a way to say to our kids: *We couldn't teach you everything. And we don't know everything. And that's okay. These are all finite skills, and you can learn them. This is the first of as many or as few of these "boot camps" or discussions about adulting as you would like. You can ask us any time.*

Holding, or even attempting to hold, these boot camps and seeing our kids go off into the world always makes clear that some things can be learned only through experience. So even if you showed your child how to do taxes when they were sixteen, they may have not gotten the message, or understood it in the way they needed to, until they're doing their own taxes for the first time. What a child learns depends on what they are ready to learn. We also take comfort that children today have access to amazing tools for learning skills without our guidance and help. YouTube exists! If a child doesn't know how to change a tire, or clear a drain, or prepare a roast chicken, they can easily find great instructional resources for any of these and many more tasks.

In an ideal world, maybe there would be a slow, steady, and smooth transition from childhood to adulthood—a program where a child incrementally takes on more financial, physical, and emotional responsibility, while slowly experiencing more time in a different home, until they finally, almost unnoticeably, move out. But while we wait for that ideal world, we've had good luck quelling our parenting panic with adulting boot camps.

4

LOOKING TO THE FUTURE

WHAT WE OWE OUR KIDS AND WHAT OUR KIDS OWE US

When we lived in Oakland,

we took an eight-week course called Marriage & Family taught by family therapist Dr. Nedra Shumway. We ended up in the class sort of randomly and didn't know what to expect, but we really enjoyed her coursework and continue to reflect on lessons we learned from that class years later.

At the end of one of the classes, Dr. Shumway told attendees that the following week we would be talking about in-laws. As we walked home from class that day we confidently said, *In-laws? That'll be easy! We both love our in-laws. We have great relationships with our in-laws. We're looking forward to the discussion.* Imagine our surprise when we walked into class the next week and realized it wasn't about our parents-in-law, it was about *us* becoming parents-in-law to our children's future partners. Up until that point, we had never really thought about this, and had not conceived of what it might be like to be parents-in-law someday.

Dr. Shumway explained that once a child becomes an adult—age eighteen in the United States—they have control of the relationship they have with you. There is an exception: If the parent is still contributing financially to the child (say, paying tuition or paying for housing), the parent still retains some control over the relationship. But if there is no financial tie, the child (now an adult) is in control. They get to decide *if* you will see them, *when* you will see them, and *how* you will see them.

If you have a crummy relationship with that child, they will likely choose to see you rarely, if ever. If they have a life partner who doesn't like you, they may choose to see you rarely, if ever. Even if you have an excellent relationship with your (now grown-up) child, you may still need to share them with another family—splitting holidays and birthdays and family trips, trading off every other year. Once they are an adult, your child will be in control of the relationship, not you.

We walked home from that class kind of stunned. For the first time, we confronted the fact that the idyllic family group we were trying so hard to cultivate was going to change dramatically, despite our best efforts. Why? Because our kids were going to become adults and forge their own lives. In fact, isn't that supposed to be the best-case scenario? That our kids grow up to have independent and happy lives? It probably shouldn't have been so shocking to us, but it was. We joked that maybe we should encourage the kids to marry orphans so that we didn't have to compete with another family for their attention.

Not long after that class, while it was still heavy on our minds, Gabrielle read an article about a son (an adult son) who was suing his parents for having been born. The son argued that he didn't ask to be born, didn't have any choice in it, and didn't particularly enjoy being alive. Contrary to what you might think, the son has an excellent relationship with his parents. They are both lawyers and contributed comments to the article about how they thought the lawsuit was interesting and admirable. Gabrielle was struck by the article and wrote a blog post about it to discuss with other parents.

After Dr. Shumway's class, the lawsuit article, and dozens of discussions we had with other parents, we came to the conclusion that children don't owe their parents anything.

We sometimes confuse the direction of responsibility between parents and children. While legally, and in our commonsense understanding, we understand that parents are responsible for the care and nurturing of their children, we also often hear about the obligations for children to respect, be thankful for, and care for their parents. We hear parents complain, *In my day, children would have never behaved like this!* . . . or we hear parents lament "difficult children." We won't contest that children should not be rude or mean to the people they interact with, including their parents, or that some children can be especially difficult—of course this can be the case. But the fact of the matter is that the direction of responsibility really goes only one way: As a parent, *you* chose to raise a child.* Your child did not choose to be born. No

---

* We're not here talking about a claim like if you chose to have sex, then you chose the consequences that go with that, including conceiving a child. That is a separate conversation. We're talking about parents who intentionally conceived in order to raise a child.

matter the sacrifices you have made to be a parent, your child doesn't owe you respect, honor, or gratitude just by virtue of being your child. Their existence is a direct result of the choices *you* made. And the fact that they were born does not make them responsible for loving you, caring for you, behaving as you would like, or being grateful for you and any sacrifices you made to be their parent. In this sense, your child doesn't "owe" you anything—respect, affection, or gratitude.

This reality plays out once a child is an adult because, as we discussed, unless a child is financially or otherwise dependent on a parent, whether you have a relationship with that child is entirely up to the child. You can't force them to call or visit or celebrate with you.

We set so many expectations for how our children will behave or respond, or what they'll be interested in, based on our own childhoods and based on what we've been taught they "owe" us. And those expectations are often a huge source of conflict. Once we understand that as parents, *we* "owe" our kids, and not the other way around, instead of assuming certain expectations, we can more easily see our kids for who they are, and identify what they need and how we can help them.

Understanding this one-way dynamic also helps us see this opportunity of parenting for the amazing thing that it is. We chose this. *We chose to have kids.* We forced them to come here and we get the joy of seeing them grow and change and become whole human beings. Who are they going to become? We have no idea! But what a treat that we get to find out, observing the whole process from a front row seat. We get to love them, care for them, find out what interests them, and see how they like to learn. We get to notice how they like to use their body and move through the world. And they're so interesting! Just sneaking in to watch them sleep when they were a baby was so compelling and interesting—and it's even more so to discover how they think and what they love as they grow.

Lastly, understanding that our kids don't owe us anything means that we have to work hard to cultivate connection (now and in the future). Of course, we hope that our child will love and appreciate us, but it is we parents who must earn this, and whether they do and what that may look like is out of our control. This is not an argument to keep your child financially dependent on you forever. Rather, it's a call to keep an image of a future slightly more distant than eighteen years in mind as you raise your child. It's an invitation to ask yourself questions like: How does your current relationship prepare for and cultivate the grounds for your relationship five, ten, or forty years beyond your child leaving the nest? When your child isn't *obligated* to have a relationship with you through their dependence on you for room and board, what would make them *want* to have a relationship with you? And what experiences can you share now that would make you both want to share more in the future, when you don't share a home?

WHY WE BELIEVE IN TAKING THE LONG VIEW

By the time this book is published, five of our six children will be adults. We didn't start our family thinking about adult children. We doubt many new parents do. As a young parent, you are consumed with caring for this helpless baby, and there is nothing in that relationship that points to their future as an adult. As parents, we're not accustomed to thinking about adult children—just try googling images for "parents" and see what percentage of the images shows parents with adult children.

Our first child moving out snuck up on us. Up to moving out, he was a daily presence and had spent nearly every night at our home for the past eighteen years (barring some concentrated weeks during holidays and in the summer), and then, abruptly, he was gone. No matter how many times we imagined him moving out, nothing compared to the actual event. Actually, each child moving out has snuck up on us. And to be frank, we haven't drastically (or incrementally) improved our send-off practices and rituals (adulting boot camp notwithstanding) so that we feel more confident with each departing child.

When we think of "parents," we think of people raising school-age kids (or younger). We don't think of the older parents of adult children. Which is probably why it comes as such a surprise that even when our kids are grown, we don't quite know what to do with our status as "parents."

As parents of young children, we weren't always aware that we were planting the seeds for our relationship with our adult children. But as they got older, we realized there was no escaping this. So together we tried to envision what a flourishing parent-child relationship would look like when our children are thirty. We're confident we'll need to update this as we and our children age, but here's what we came up with:

We have a full, meaningful, free-flowing, noncoercive relationship with our children. We understand and respect one another's boundaries. We are all independent, but we enjoy one another's company. We value one another and the experiences we've shared, even if some experiences were painful. Without sugarcoating our time together, we deeply appreciate and trust one another. We can work easily with one another on a range of projects across a range of spheres, over extended periods of time. We have a good understanding of one another's strengths and weaknesses. We communicate easily with one another. We ask for advice and ask to hear one another's perspective. We appreciate what we have learned from one another. We can challenge, disagree, and debate, but these don't threaten our relationship, even as our relationship is dynamic and continues to develop and change over time.

We recognize that parenting rightly centers on these critical early years before a child has launched—this is when children need parents. But our image of launching—where a child moves out of the house, and should thereafter be emotionally and financially independent—is proving inaccurate and unsustainable—for both the child and the parents. Add to this that more things are changing faster today than ever before, and the problems with a model of parenting based on outdated benchmarks and pathways can lead to crises for children and parents and their relationship.

As we've tried to imagine a full, meaningful, free-flowing relationship with our adult children (even while some are not yet adults), we've also tried to imagine what we could do today that would prepare the way for that future. We try to be aware of the influence of our own childhood experiences on our outlook as people, and especially as parents. We try to have open conversations with each child about their hopes, fears, and aspirations, and, to the extent they want to, continue those conversations once they become adults. We have tried to share a wide variety of experiences together—both for the satisfaction they bring now, and for the groundwork and precedence they provide for more shared experiences later. We now talk more frequently about themes like what parents owe children, the reliable path to success, implications of the accelerating pace of change, including our growing uncertainty about the future, and, in light of all this, what a healthy, long-term parent-child relationship looks like.

As parents, we're aiming to raise independent people who can thrive, even without a straightforward path, and even in an uncertain and rapidly evolving future. And most important, we're aiming to cultivate lasting, flourishing relationships that develop and extend throughout life.

ACKNOWLEDGMENTS

This book has been influenced by too many to name, but we can't neglect to mention at least a few:

We want to thank our children, Ralph, Maude, Olive, Oscar, Betty, and Flora June. We are so grateful to have had a front-row seat to your lives.

Thank you to our agent, Meg Thompson, who helped shepherd the book proposal into a compelling idea, and who had our backs whenever we had naive author questions.

Thank you to our publisher, Lia Ronnen, who pushed us to write a parenting book and made us feel like essential voices when we felt we had no business writing about parenting.

Thank you to our editor, Maisie Tivnan. We sent Maisie the roughest rough draft of a manuscript that you can conceive of, and she went back and forth with us for many months, clarifying ideas, simplifying the structure, and shaping it into the book you are now reading.

Thank you to all the fine folks at Workman Publishing. Thanks to production editor Beth Levy, for helping us get things right. To Becky Terhune, who oversaw the layout and indulged our opinions. To Barbara Peragine, who did the typesetting and accommodated our edits. Thanks to the marketing and publicity team: Rebecca Carlisle, Moira Kerrigan, Ilana Gold, and Allison McGeehon, for helping us better see and extend a hand to potential readers. Thank you to David Schiller for the many title brainstorming sessions. We're aware there are lots of other hands at Workman that this book passed through and who helped bring it to the world. We may not know their names, but we're grateful for them.

Thank you to the legendary Bonnie Siegler, who created the design for this book—both the cover and the interior. It was a pleasure and a distinct honor to work with her again. We gasped when we saw the cover design and every page felt elevated by her touch.

Thank you to Lindsay Edgecombe, who we worked with for an earlier book proposal that eventually became this book and whose feedback is still manifest.

Thank you to our good friend Avi Mintz, for encouraging comments when the book was mostly an idea and for gracious feedback and insightful challenges on an early draft.

Thank you to Parenting Gonzales.

Thank you to our parents: Ben's parents, Bob and Julia Blair, and Gabrielle's father, Mike Stanley, have passed away, but we feel their imprint on the steps we have taken as parents and the lessons that have organized this book. And thank you to Gabrielle's mother, Donna Stanley McEvoy, whose imprint is also throughout, and who has been, and remains, a constant giver of confidence throughout Gabrielle's full life, and our entire married life.

Lastly, thank you to *Design Mom* readers who have shared your hopes and concerns for eighteen years—reflecting on what you have shared has fueled this book. And thank you to Newlane University students and teachers who have shared their experiences—especially surrounding false promises of "the reliable path to success"—and whose examples have demonstrated again and again the possibility and value of alternative paths.

ABOUT THE AUTHORS

Ben Blair holds a PhD in Philosophy and Education from Columbia University. He is a cofounder and president of Newlane University. Started in 2017, Newlane is an online university with a mission to make quality liberal arts higher education accessible to anyone on earth by breaking down barriers of cost, schedule, and geography. Newlane students and professors are based in 40+ different countries. Newlane offers affordable, accredited Bachelor's degrees.

Gabrielle Blair is the founder of DesignMom .com. Started in 2006, it has been named a Parenting Website of the Year by *Time* magazine, and praised as a top parenting blog by *The Wall Street Journal*, *Parents*, and *Better Homes and Gardens*. Gabrielle is also a founder of Alt Summit, the blockbuster annual conference for creatives and creative entrepreneurs who work online, currently in its sixteenth year. As a thought leader for more than eighteen years, Gabrielle's writing is quoted and shared across the globe daily.

Gabrielle's most recent book, *Ejaculate Responsibly: A Whole New Way to Think About Abortion*, an instant *New York Times* bestseller, was published in 2022 by Workman, and is available in twelve international editions.

Ben and Gabrielle have six children: Ralph, Maude, Olive, Oscar, Betty, and Flora June. After six years in Oakland, California, they now live in Normandy, France, where they are renovating a home built in the 1400s. You can follow along at @DesignMom on Instagram.